HOW TO UNDERSTAND ⌐

In this Series

Other titles in preparation

UNDERSTAND
FINANCE AT WORK

A guide to better management and decision-making

Peter Marshall
BSc(Econ) BA FRSA FSBT MIM

How To Books

By the same author
How to Master Book-Keeping

British Library cataloguing-in-publication data
A catalogue record for this book is available from the British Library.

© 1994 by Peter Marshall.

First published in 1994 by How To Books Ltd, Plymbridge House, Estover Road, Plymouth PL6 7PZ, United Kingdom. Tel: Plymouth (0752) 735251/695745. Fax: (0752) 695699. Telex: 45635.

Note: The material contained in this book is set out in good faith for general guidance and no liability can be accepted for loss or expense incurred as a result of relying in particular circumstances on statements made in the book. The laws and regulations are complex and liable to change, and readers should check the current position with the relevant authorities before making personal arrangements.

Typeset by PDQ Typesetting, Stoke-on-Trent
Printed and bound by The Cromwell Press, Broughton Gifford, Melksham, Wiltshire.

Contents

List of Illustrations

Preface

In this climate of great economic change there is a need for a 'bang-up-to-date' book on finance, which is accessible even to people who normally avoid the subject. A book which can really claim to be up-to-date must recognise and provide for the profound changes which are taking place in the way human welfare is funded not only in the UK but throughout the industrialised world.

More people are going to have to stand on their own feet. Increasingly, welfare services previously provided by the state and funded through taxation will become funded on the basis of 'risk for profit' in the private sector. This will require increased financial awareness among the population, as more and more people fund their existence by their own enterprise, and as almost every conceivable public service, once managed by the state, has to take responsibility for itself.

It's not only knowledge and skills which must be quickly learned. Attitudes, too, must change. Long-standing institutional attitudes, appropriate for conditions of the past, must now be discarded faster than they were acquired, as the circumstances for which they were appropriate are disappearing overnight. Consequently, this book targets financial attitudes, too. It reveals the real meanings and rationale underlying the obsolete and the newly emerging financial values and arrangements.

It is aimed at students and business people alike. In the knowledge and skills section it is designed to be as comprehensive but user-friendly as possible. I have avoided going into too much detail on accounts – my other book, *How to Master Book-Keeping*, serves that purpose and I have, on occasions, cross-referenced.

So whether you work in a large or small organisation, or are still preparing for a future career, it is hoped that this book will set you thinking critically about such issues as accountability, efficiency, development and change. I hope too that it will help you play your part – as we all must – in constantly finding better ways of financing our social and business needs in the future.

Peter Marshall

1
Managing Change

ADAPTING AND SURVIVING

As social environments change, their inhabitants evolve and those which adapt best survive. Nature carries no passengers for long. And in our modern concrete jungle Nature is no less ruthless than in the wild.

But how must we adapt? We absorb knowledge, learn skills and develop attitudes to cope with particular conditions, but when those times change we must adapt ourselves.

Changing our way of thinking

Knowledge and skills are easy enough to update – it's old attitudes which lag behind, and those who stick to them most rigidly will be among the losers in the struggle. Those whose minds are most flexible, most ready to grasp the nettle of change and adapt to it will be among the winners. That's what distinguishes winners and losers, and the race is getting more competitive every day: not simply for individuals, but for organisations of every shape and size, geographical regions, and whole nations.

Attitudes are understandably hard to change because we've grown up with them – they're all we know. We tend to believe they're absolutely right for all time, but they're really only mental organising tools, they orientate us towards our environment in the most appropriate way, motivating us to do this, learn that, avoid this, or behave like that. When our environment changes, our attitudes too must be changed, as we struggle to develop a new way of thinking.

It's tempting to imagine ourselves still in those times when competition, financial responsibility, profit and material things seemed less important. A new, intensely market-orientated world is now challenging us, full of risks. The old world was a sweet place, but it belongs in the past.

All but a small minority of human beings in the modern industrial world spend most of their waking hours in the production or exchange of goods and services, and the environment in which that takes place is a ruthlessly financial one. Finance is the very air it breathes. And just as those afraid of the water will drown if thrown into it, those who are afraid of their financial environment will perish too.

GRASPING THE NETTLE OF CHANGE

In the last few years, the whole world has been catapulted into a new phase of history, social and economic, in which the market is the supreme dynamic. It has new kinds of problems demanding new kinds of answers. The effects are felt everywhere, and perhaps most noticeably in the public sector.

Firms are increasingly having to replace labour with machinery to keep production costs down, but the job losses lead to an ever-growing population of unemployed dependants on the state welfare services. This puts an increasingly high burden on Western taxpayers. If investors are taxed too highly on their profits from local firms they will transfer their funds overseas, causing even more jobs to be lost.

We are having to shift the burden of funding 'public' services onto private sector entrepreneurs. Along with the burden goes the risk, so they will want a profit.

Another consequence of the changing conditions is that firms are less able to afford the welfare benefits they had once guaranteed for their employees, eg specific pay levels and redundancy payments. This is because Third World countries are now entering the market-place, and their prices do not include such burdens.

How the world of finance and investment is changing

We can summarise the types of changes taking place as follows:

- New sources of funding for welfare services.

- New sources of funding for other state provisions.

- Change from planning to market criteria.

- Shifting the risk involved in the provision of public works and services from the public sector to the private sector.

- Putting the control of production and consumption back into the hands of the people, by means of the price mechanism.

Consequently we are seeing:
- State provision going private, eg gas, electricity, telephone services and soon the railways.

- Re-privatisation of nationalised industries.

- New roles for Local Authorities (enabling rather than providing).

- Contracting out of state-provided services, eg Liverpool's City Clean, providing refuse services.

- Franchising, eg railway lines.

- Commercial operating agreements to developers, eg the proposed Northern Bypass.

- Many dependent on state support are being encouraged to stand on their own feet, becoming risk-takers themselves, eg the Enterprise Allowance Scheme and The Prince's Youth Business Trust.

Why are these changes taking place?
The reasons can be summarised like this:

- Too heavy a burden on the taxpayer.

- Need to reduce the national debt.

- Civil servants are not the best people to estimate the risks (entrepreneurs are).

- Risks should actually be paid for by profit.

- Consumers can more effectively communicate their wants through price.

- Market forces result in greater efficiency.

The drive for efficiency also brings numerous other changes of a technological nature. These are conspicuous for example in the way we use banks, including the use of home banking by computer, or touch-sensitive phone pads. Coming into force shortly are the new 'Smart Cards' which will automatically bill customers for such things as road usage.

UNDERSTANDING THE NEEDS AND OPPORTUNITIES CHANGE BRINGS

All change brings new needs and opportunities. Those who merely complain about the changes will stagnate and, perhaps, even perish financially. Those who see them as challenges will prosper.

Needs on an institutional level include:

- Creative answers to old, worsening problems.

- New political conceptions regarding welfare.

- Need for new sources of funds and new candidates to bear the risks, in the provision of public services.

- Lower taxation and other incentives to people to bear the risk.

- More efficient methods of provision – profit incentives.

- These will require new kinds of institutions:
  – Enabling authorities.
  – Private welfare provision.

- More mentorship schemes, training schemes, business establishment schemes.

Needs at an individual level:
- A greater proportion of people willing to stand on their own feet – more self-employment opportunities. This means fostering a new self-respect and sense of personal responsibility among people, especially the young.

- More individual investors in enterprise.

- A new breed of market-orientated civil servants.

- A new breed of school governors.

- A new breed of entrepreneurial academics.

- A new breed of health service chiefs.

- A new breed of entrepreneurial GPs.

- More productivity per unit of labour to compete with foreign firms.

- More investment by foreign firms.

- New skill training opportunities.

- Possibilities for real new earnings.

- New business mentorship for opportunities for the young, like The Prince's Youth Business Trust (PYBT).

New product needs
New efficiency needs bring new market opportunities, for example in these areas:

- Private health insurance.

- Unemployment insurance.

- Legal fees insurance.

- Educational endowment policies.

- New methods of charging for services, eg smart cards for road usage.

- Point of sale banking, on-line accounting systems and so on.

The changes can be viewed as obstacles or opportunities. Those who see them as the latter are likely to be the ones who will equip themselves to exploit them. The more they are needed the more financial reward they will offer. That's the way the market regulates supply and demand.

SHEDDING THE MUNICIPAL MENTALITY

The eventual withering away of the state bureaucracy has always been seen as a goal on both sides of the political fence – capitalist and communist. In Marxist theory it is the crucial goal; in capitalist theory the ideal is that state provision should amount to no more than a legal system for the enforcement of debts and the prevention of fraud and a policy which prevents monopolies arising.

There are two noticeable ways the provision of welfare services can be arranged and organised – on **market criteria** and on **political criteria**.

- Provision based on market criteria is motivated by the people's own preferences, as shown by the relative prices they are prepared to pay for different goods and services. This benefits them primarily in that it serves to satisfy their maximum wants.

- Provision based on political criteria is motivated by the political aspirations of the bureaucrats, encouraging some practices and discouraging others, favouring some supply firms and neglecting others, according to whether their values and practices match the political preferences of the bureaucrats. It represents a hijacking of life's natural system of provision and want-satisfaction for use as a powerful political tool.

The municipality is not the right social organ for risk; that belongs in the private sector – civil servants have neither the training, instinct nor motivation to develop the expertise. Placing risk in the public sector is an anomaly.

When an economy is organised in a micro way (with many firms satisfying needs in the free market) then faults in the system have small consequences. However, when certain goods and services are produced for the whole society by a monolithic state organisation faults have great and costly consequences.

In our society the large and clumsy bureaucracy of municipal provision grew up in a time when economic conditions were very different from what they are today. In the 1960s there was an economic boom, unemployment was low, and earnings were high. There was plenty of revenue, without diminishing disposable incomes to unacceptable levels. By the mid-1970s state provision had become so large and burdensome, that diseconomies of scale were taking place – red tape was one of the problems. Furthermore, under state provision supply and consumption were being used as political tools, encouraging certain practices and discouraging others, favouring some organisations at the expense of others.

In every sector of life there are set attitudes to adopt; they do, in the main, defend the status quo of that sector. In the civil service they have tended to favour municipal provision.

The benefits of competition

It's competition, though, that will always ensure the best allocation of resources, and this means the cheapest supply of goods and services. But competition means risk-taking and nobody is going to do that for nothing; there has to be a pay-off, there has to be a profit. But since all available wit, strength and skill will be used in the competitive action, just as in the organic jungle, the costs will be kept to a minimum and the products will be available at the lowest cost.

It didn't matter much to individual civil servants; it wasn't their money that was being used, it was the taxpayers' and ratepayers'. The system gave them a lot of power; after all, they were able to direct the consuming behaviour of others by saying what would be produced, a decision which should have rightly been the consumers' own. But it didn't allocate resources efficiently; it didn't produce goods and services at minimum cost to the people.

State provision never does. The Soviet Union example profoundly demonstrated that and even China is beginning to veer away from a paternalistic, planned economy system. When the old guard, with their entrenched attitudes, finally die out we will probably see a much more vigorous return to a competitive system. (And that, of course, will mean even more competition for the West.)

Adapting our ways of thinking

Successful people have flexible minds and recognise attitudes for what they are, adaptations to conditions. They recognise when they have become obsolete, when times have changed. They don't doggedly hold on to attitudes developed to cope with the conditions of yesterday. They 'grasp the nettle' that we have moved on into another phase, and new, more appropriate, attitudes have to be formed or adopted. Attitudes are never right or wrong in absolute terms, only more or less appropriate. The young tend to manage this flexibility more than the old; the old communist guards in China serve as an example again. This is why companies tend to practise what is often, of late, termed as ageism, so whatever your age if you want to survive convince your employer you can move with the times.

DEVELOPING AN ENTERPRISE OUTLOOK

Financing the production of goods and services in a way which
involves risk will always call for the utmost efficiency, and optimum
employment of resources – no wastage of resources or energy. Risk-
taking behaviour progresses towards perfection. In contrast,
financing without risk leads to waste in every way. Think about it.
What is there to restrain it beyond an agreed level? In the
competitive system every penny that can be knocked off price will
attract more sales and more personal profit, so both sides gain,
consumers and producers. When you accept these arguments you
have begun to develop an enterprise outlook.

Privatisation

More and more state services are being privatised. If the new owners
and managers don't use their money efficiently, giving the best value
for money, someone else will and they will disappear. The electricity,
gas and water supplies and the telephone service have all gone into the
private sector already. Soon some of the roads and railways will follow
and new ways will continue to be found to subject what remains to
market forces, even those services which would have seemed
unthinkable candidates for privatisation a few years ago. Adam
Smith, in *Wealth of Nations* (1776), on which our modern market
economy is based, saw the provision of the legal system for the
prevention of fraud and the enforcement of debts and an agency to
prevent the emergence of monopolies as the only ways in which it was
justified for a government to intervene in the free market system. In the
end, probably every service that can conceivably be provided by the
private sector will be shed from the state's responsibility.

The trend back towards the private provision of welfare services
began when Local Authorities began to contract out, by competitive
tender, services which had formerly been provided directly by them.
They also began to form partnerships with private companies.
Things have moved on since then and in the end Local Authorities
will become simply enabling authorities, rather than providers,
making things possible, stimulating and monitoring the private
provision of everything the people need.

If we believe in a market economy we should not deprive the people
of market opportunities (for either supplying or consuming) by
snatching away into municipal hands the supply of certain products
and services which the market can take care of directly itself.

Furthermore, it is wrong to expect the public to take the risks when professional risk-takers exist in the market.

Advantages of the market
Advantages of the market are:

- Competition results in lower prices.

- Incentives to bring out new products and to increase efficiency.

- Price mechanism is a handy *nature given* regulator and will allocate resources efficiently free of charge.

- Freedom to buy and sell any products or services (with only certain exceptions for the public good, eg drugs, firearms and hard porn).

- Freedom to work in any occupation because market price matches supply with demand for labour.

- The number of state officials is reduced and this means less wastage of labour resources. This also expands the supply of labour, thus reducing labour price and, indirectly, the price of goods.

- People can choose what they want to be produced with the country's resources by deciding what they are prepared to pay for it.

- Civil servants are not the best business people, they have no experience or special training in risk-taking.

Do you have an enterprise outlook?
Elements of an enterprise outlook feature:

- Feeling positive about enterprise.

- Recognition that civil servants have neither the motive nor the expertise to handle risk.

- Belief in enterprise as an answer to the funding problem.

- Belief in competition as a means of increasing efficiency.

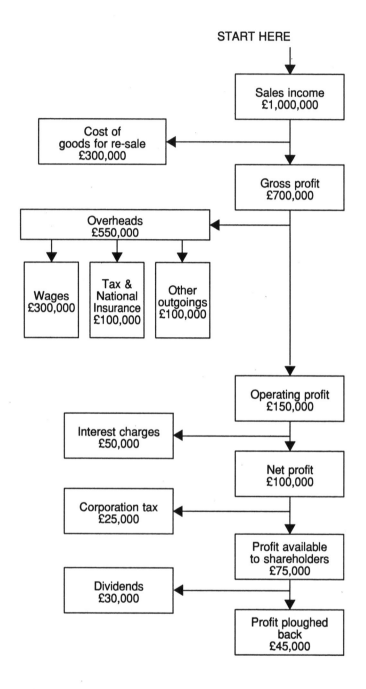

Fig. 1. Where the profit goes in a trading firm (typical example).

- Recognition of the failure of the old municipal way of providing.

- Awareness of the stimulus to investment arising from easing the burden on the taxpayer and the benefit of this to all as a means of increasing jobs.

- Having too much self-respect to want to be dependent on others.

- The belief that everyone of able body and mind should stand on his or her own feet.

- Not being afraid of risk and hard work.

- Being confident and brave enough to make his or her success depend on his or her own merits, rather than on an institutional power.

- Belief that the public should be free to choose what they want produced with the country's resources and that the price mechanism is the best means of communicating this.

- Belief that whenever a way can be found to release state provisions of goods and services into the private sector it should be done.

- Acceptance that it is wrong, and detrimental to the people, to deprive them of the *price eroding* effect of market forces upon the goods and services which they consume by supplying them under the state provision instead.

MAKING FRIENDS WITH PROFIT

We've got to get over this attitude still held by some people that profit is somehow tainted or wrong. It isn't and we'll soon see why. But first let's establish what profit actually is.

Profit means the return for risk. Nobody takes a risk for nothing. No one will back the horses if there's no prize to be gained, so why should anyone back a business venture if there's no reward?

Calculating 'profit'

In essence it's easy to define, but when it comes to calculating how much profit has been made, things are not so clear-cut. There are two basic ways to evaluate how much profit has been earned:

- Increase in net assets. Example: net assets on 1st January £10,000. Net assets on 31st December £17,000. Profit for period – £7,000.

- Deducting outgoings from income. Example: income £120,000, outgoings £40,000. Profit £80,000.

However, different people may well arrive at different figures whichever way it's calculated. This is because estimates have to be made about such things as erosion or increase in asset values. Inflation confuses the issue further. Also, the amount of bad debt the firm may have to write off cannot be known in advance; estimates have to be made of this. Different people make different judgements about all these things. So just because one might calculate profit as one figure and another arrive at another, it doesn't mean one is wrong and the other is right. The test of acceptability of a profit figure is whether it is regarded fair to all parties concerned – the shareholders, the company and the Inland Revenue – and even that is difficult to judge. Furthermore, 'creative accounting' can result in the profit figure reported not representing a true and fair view at all.

Surpluses, drawings, and profits

All organisations would prefer to end up with a surplus of revenue over expenditure than a deficit – that's just a case of good housekeeping, where careful expenditure results in lower than predicted costs. But this surplus is only called a 'profit' if it is regarded as the rightful reward to the financial risk-taker who invested his or her money in the enterprise in the first place.

Nor is profit simply the income from supplying goods or services, as some business people would appear to think when they refer to this income as earnings. It's not earnings at all; some of it has to be used to pay suppliers and overhead expenses. Only that which is left over when all costs are finally met is profit earned.

Nor are a small business person's weekly or monthly drawings really profits, as many mistakenly think of them. How can they be? They don't know whether they'll make a profit for the year until it's over. A surplus of income over expenditure one day may be followed by a deficit the next. It's only really meaningful to talk of profit over a period, such as the trading year. After all, that's what a business person will by law be taxed upon. Drawings should more realistically be regarded as withdrawals of capital; if a profit is made over the trading year the profit will replenish that capital.

Profitability: the ability to make a profit

Profitability is more important than absolute profits since it relates to the amount invested. A company which has made £1,000,000 profit from investing £2,000,000 has done much better than one which has made £2,000,000 but on an investment of £8,000,000. **Return on capital employed** is a more useful barometer of success than profit.

Consistency of profits is more important to investors than sudden peaks, but sometimes companies may actually plan to make short-term losses when such endeavours would bring them long-term profits.

Opportunity cost

It's misleading to assume that to invest £10,000 in a business venture which will return you £12,000 in a year's time gives you a reward of £2,000 or twenty per cent for your risk. You could have gained, say, eight per cent on your capital – £800 – by taking virtually no risk at all, leaving the money earning interest in a building society account. So it is perhaps more realistic to say your reward for placing it in the business venture instead amounts to only twelve per cent, ie from the profit of £2,000 you make you must deduct your **opportunity cost** (the opportunity of making eight per cent or £800 in a safe investment).

Profits, dividends and reserves

Dividends paid to shareholders are strictly speaking their profits on their investments. But dividends represent only part of the company's profits, some of which will have had to be paid in taxes, some probably transferred to capital reserve to finance growth, and some probably held on profit and loss account to help meet day-to-day expenses.

Misconceptions

Surely rising sales means rising profits?
No, not at all. The increase may be due to reduced prices, greater expenditure on selling expenses, or poor credit vetting, in which case profits may even decline.

Surely bargain buying opportunities will inevitably lead to increased profits?
No, not at all. It may well mean overstocking, which means money

is tied up, storage costs are excessive and goods may perish. There may also be interest to pay on finance used to stock up. Even if none of these are the case the increased stocking of bargain priced goods will have an opportunity cost in that money used for them will not be able to be used for other goods and the profit which would be earned from the latter must be deducted as an opportunity cost.

Profit and cash are the same things?
They are not. No matter how profitable your sales are, if your cash is flowing in slower than it is flowing out, eg if your customers pay you more slowly than you pay your suppliers, you'll run out of cash, suppliers will stop supplying you and you'll go under.

Shrinking market
The world market is shrinking. Third World countries, who in the past were largely consumers, are now entering on the supply end. Their production costs are low because of low wages and welfare benefits in those countries. On the other hand a consequential depression in the home economy has led to a much heavier state burden of welfare support. There is little money in the public purse to develop the country's infrastructure. Increased taxes will only reduce investment and consumption further, and so new ways of funding state provision have to be found.

The **factor market** is the natural source, neglected for so long. Funding for formerly state provision is now, and will increasingly be, sought from private firms in return for the reward of profit. Maximum privatisation holds the key. The state need provide only the bare minimum of facilitating, stimulating and monitoring services.

The morality of profit
The often-heard view that 'profit is immoral' is Marxist. The Marxist view is that it's wrong for entrepreneurs to 'cream off' the fruits of a person's labour, but this view is misguided.

It's remotely conceivable that a single street musician can provide his service by the investment of his labour alone (and the negligible cost of the harmonica), but in the production of most goods and services there will be more than labour going into it. The profit comes from the **added value** that resources gain when they're put together in a certain way.

For example when wood and labour are put together in a building hired as a workshop for the time needed to make a table. . . the product is worth more in the market-place than the sum of the inputs. The surplus is due, in part, to all the *inputs*, not just the labour. If someone agreed to bear the risk of it making a loss, without which it would not have been made, then he, too, deserves a bit of it. So you see, profit cannot be 'wrong'. The landlord is paid rent for his input into the production process; the workers are paid wages for putting in their time and effort; the entrepreneurs or investors who have taken the financial risk are likewise entitled to be paid for their service and their payment is known as profit.

Nobody gambles for nothing. Many a working man will gamble a proportion of his wages on the horses each week. He could, instead, gamble it on the stock market, ie investing in companies; it's really no different. Business ventures involve risk and professional gamblers are the experts with risk. If a worker bets his money on horses he expects a reward; he wouldn't do it for nothing, so why should an entrepreneur? Moreover the entrepreneur who buys company shares also helps to protect workers' jobs.

The importance of profit

- Investors won't invest without the hope of profits.
- Profit is a measure of performance.
- Profit induces risk-taking without which the market economy would stagnate and jobs would be lost.
- Profit prevents takeovers and asset-stripping, and helps prevent job losses.
- Profits provide taxes for social needs.
- Profits provide the money to maintain and develop infrastructure.
- Profits provide for reinvestment to finance growth.
- Profits provide short-term funds to meet day-to-day expenses.

So off with the old, on with the new. The Government is promoting an enterprise culture, and what is needed is an enterprise outlook. We've got to put behind us any reservations we have about profit. The whole financial world is changing, and a few years from now will have become almost unrecognisable.

LIVING WITH COMPETITION

Competition is the law of the jungle and reigns every bit as supreme in the human world as in the animal one. Any attempts to replace it with state-controlled economic activity amounts only to nationwide withdrawal from reality; the Soviet Union experience demonstrated that. Every community must in the end stand on its own feet and be prepared to struggle to survive. We have the ability to observe that attitudes, skills and knowledge will enable us to compete favourably with others and we have the ability to develop these in ourselves, sharpening up our fitness to survive.

Playing to win

Surviving in the modern market system is a big game; there are rules to restrain excessive impulses. Not everyone is playing the same game though; there are levels at which we choose to compete. Just as in sports competitions, we assess our competence level and enter the most appropriate division of the league, where we know we will have a reasonable chance of winning. It's knowing the level at which to set our sights which protects our self-esteem – set it too high and we'll destroy ourselves; too low and we'll achieve the same effect. You'll never see a ferret attack a lion, but the ferret nearly always wins his game because he knows which league to compete in.

But enter we must. If we sit on the sidelines, or worse still, avoid the game, protesting that it is 'wrong', we fool nobody but ourselves. The game will go on whether we like it or not, as it has for millions of years in one form or another. If you want to be a lemming in the market-place, go ahead, nobody will stop you, they'll all be too busy playing their own game.

If we are going to finance what were formerly state provisions by using professional investors who will take the risks for a profit, then we must make the *game* fair, so that the winners and losers achieve their results by their own merits, without any unequal help from the system or through use of monopolistic power. The discerning consumer seeks out the best value for money and so prices are forced down. The firm who can offer the lowest price for the same goods and services wins.

Understanding the international dimension

Countries compete against each other, too. Governments must try to export at least as much as (and hopefully more than) they import. Otherwise they will suffer a **balance of payments** disequilibrium. This must then be resolved by borrowing or currency devaluation. Consequently, governments actively encourage firms and employees to be as competitive as possible. Firms should keep pay increases low, and employees discouraged from using monopolistic power of strikes and other trade union activity to push through price-damaging pay deals. On an individual level employees must sell their labour in the 'factor' market (this refers to the buying and selling of the four factors of production – land, labour, capital and enterprise). Those who offer firms best value for money will find jobs quickest.

Competition from the East
In the Third World countries, low wages and lack of welfare commitments enable them to keep their prices very low. Western firms – and Japan – are being forced to replace labour with machines, to keep their prices low enough to compete. Unless they really do compete, they will lose sales, make losses, go broke and everyone will lose their jobs. Even if firms don't actually run into loss, if profits are not as high as in other firms shareholders will sell their shares, and when share prices fall below the assets value they represent, a predatory firm may well buy them up, sell off the assets piecemeal for a quick profit, close down the firm and everyone will still lose their jobs. It's not simply because firms are becoming more 'greedy' that they're having to lay people off – they have no choice if the rest are to survive.

One effect of staff reductions is that the supply side of the home factor market is swelled, as displaced workers look for new jobs. Competition for jobs becomes even fiercer and workers have to look even better to prospective employers to have a chance of being chosen.

Since the 1940s we've grown weak and helpless in a paternalistic economy; our welfare has been so assured that we could all but forget our survival skills. But such a cushioning society is costly to maintain. The costs of supporting fellow citizens through non-productive periods like holidays, illness and unemployment add much to the costs of the goods produced by the rest. This worked while world demand outstripped supply, because people were prepared to pay the inflated prices for goods which they could not otherwise obtain. Once the Third World started to join the producers, though – and without carrying the burdens of financing welfare benefits out of the proceeds – the goods produced in the Western world began to price themselves out of the market. However much people may condemn countries who exploit the labour of their people without providing welfare benefits, they themselves will still, in the main, choose to buy the cheaper, Third World goods.

The age factor
Added to this pressure people are living longer than they used to.

This means more and more are becoming dependent on fewer and fewer people. While we still embrace the value of providing welfare services to those who are not able to provide for themselves we really owe it to everyone to do it as efficiently as possible. It's been plain for a long, long time that running services by means of state bureaucracies has given poor value for money. Welfare services must be opened up to market forces.

SPEAKING THE LANGUAGE OF FINANCE

The production of goods and services has to be financed, whether in the market system or otherwise. But in the market system 'finance' plays an additional role. As well as simply paying for factors of production, it also acts as a language – it communicates demand for particular things to providers of them, whether they are selling land usage (landlords), money (banks), labour (employees) or taking risks (investors). If demand is high, price will become high. On the other hand, if few forestry workers are needed the wages offered will be rather low. Firms and consumers communicate how much they want a commodity by the price they are prepared to pay for it. The most successful firms are those who are most receptive and sensitive to this language of price and best able to grasp what it's telling them.

Using financial terminology

Indeed, financial literacy is so important in our fast-moving industrial world that if we want to be taken seriously we have to get to grips with it. We have to learn the lingo. Not only is it used for the purposes mentioned above but it's also used to measure performance, efficiency and viability, it's used in investment appraisal and for deferring payments. Indeed, finance is a universal language in which every aspect of business activity is expressed, recorded, evaluated, measured, interpreted and communicated. Here are some everyday financial terms with which we need to be familiar:

- profit
- gross profit
- net profit
- cash flow

- break-even point
- current assets
- fixed assets
- depreciation.

Each of these terms has a clear meaning, understood by everyone concerned with finance – and not just accountants, bank managers and entrepreneurs, but managers of every kind working in almost every kind of public or private organisation. We will come to this in more detail in chapters 3 and 4.

LEARNING TO STAND ON OUR OWN FEET

We are entering an era when our society will no longer be able to afford to carry as many passengers. Guaranteed livelihoods will soon be a thing of the past. The vast majority will be responsible for supporting their own existence. The shoring up of failing industries by state subsidies will become a thing of the past. Indeed, there is no such thing as a true 'state subsidy' in our kind of society; the 'subsidy' is simply money taken from the people who are producing, earning and paying tax. Failing industries which are shored up by state subsidies are certainly not 'standing on their own feet'.

'Safe havens'

The civil service used to be a 'safe bet', a more or less guaranteed existence (and inflation-proofed retirement) financed by the taxes of others. 'Get into there and you've got a job for life,' parents used to say. Why? Because it was cushioned from the real world – inward looking, self-perpetuating, highly defensive, and civil servants wielded a lot of power, so were well placed to defend their fortresses.

It isn't a safe bet any more. Civil servants are suddenly finding they are being catapulted into the private sector – the jungle of market forces and economic reality. But just as a dolphin reared in captivity will be vulnerable if suddenly released into the ocean, so will the newly freed civil servants in the market place. Like the dolphin they must learn to survive by their own efforts very quickly indeed. The skills and knowledge can in fact all be learned relatively quickly; it's the *attitudes* which lag behind.

Others, too, are being coaxed by market forces out of their safe havens to support their own existence – the unemployed. The financing of their existence came from the market in the final analysis anyway, except that it was channelled through the state. It is people competing successfully in the market who fund the existence of the unemployed, as their incomes and profits are taxed to pay for it. Furthermore, unemployed people represent immense unused resources in the production process.

Opportunities for profitable self-employment

A society like ours can support both large and small firms. It's often unfeasible for large firms to produce small stocks of highly specialised components they need for their production processes; their production lines are too large and inflexible. These big organisations provide a market for small firms which many of those hitherto unemployed could establish.

How some people are standing on their own feet

- State teacher – now runs education and training consultancy

- Sales representative – now runs own independent sales force

- Manager – now runs own business as a result of a 'management buyout' from his former employer

- Department store manager – now runs own small specialist retail business

- Redundant bus driver – now runs own commercial vehicle hire business

- Engineer – now patenting and marketing own specialist technical product

- Unemployed linguist – now running courses on business languages for exporters

If there are opportunities in the market for such people why are they supported by others? One reason may be that they have had no apprenticeship in surviving in the business jungle. Even wild animals in the jungle get that, under the protection of their parents. However, organisations like The Prince's Youth Business Trust and the Enterprise Allowance Schemes, whereby fledgling entrepreneurs can be weaned gradually away from their guaranteed subsistence and given a range of training and mentorship facilities, provide some of the answer to this.

Even the severely handicapped can provide for themselves to some degree. A novel scheme was recently established in Cardiff, for example, whereby handicapped workers would provide the labour on a herb farm, giving them a more interesting life than remaining inside an institution, and at the same time helping to fund their own existence.

ACCEPTING RISK

What is risk? It's a fact of life and if we don't take risks for ourselves, others have to take them for us. Willingness to take reasonable risks is a mark of maturity and our new social and economic conditions will require that everyone from eighteen onwards must grow up and take responsibility for themselves. Risk-taking is a willingness to act without full knowledge and understanding of all the conditions.

It's also what regular punters on the horses, pools participants and bingo players do all the time. But much of that is done almost blindfolded; few of the conditions are known, and the outcomes are very hard to predict. Many of those same people would regard taking any such risk in respect of their livelihoods as to be avoided at all costs. There are two explanations for this:

1. While the odds are far greater in those purely sporting wagers they can still be recklessly bold when not much is at stake. In contrast, risks relating to their livelihood, while much more predictable, involve a much greater loss if miscalculated.

2. While the bigger, more dangerous risks still have to be taken anyway, up to now it's been possible to avoid them and let someone else take them for us.

But we're entering a time when people will have to be more prepared to take responsibility for assessing the environment, taking careful stock of their own knowledge, skills and abilities, the costs, the benefits and the risks, making careful judgements for action and then having the courage to act on them and accept all of the consequences, without complaint, whether they be good or bad. The earth owes none of us a living; all species – man, animal and plant – if they want an existence, have to carve it out for themselves.

Fortunately, it's not essential for us to win every time anyway, as long as we win more times than we lose. Our mistakes are valuable lessons to learn by; we don't learn without them. If we are afraid of losing we will never be winners because we'll deprive ourselves of both the chance and the lessons. Being afraid to lose is a good way of ensuring we do so.

CASE STUDIES: COPING WITH CHANGE

Theresa, the leisure industry manager

Theresa L'Pralm is a 40 year old managing director of a holding company in the leisure industry. She read economics at university, took a diploma in management studies and then went to work for a travel agency as a trainee in the accounts department. She became office manager by the age of 29, progressed through a number of job changes to Financial Director, before taking up her present post.

She knows well the crucial importance of firm financial control. She keeps up to date on all financial aspects of economic life, both at home and abroad, and sees all change as full of potential opportunity. She is a fair-minded woman, but holds no illusions about life – someone has to pay the bills at all levels; there are no free rides.

Ralph, the health authority manager

Ralph Elmaster is a 55 year old General Manager of a District Health Authority. He has been employed in the NHS all his working life and joined because of the security it offered. But things have changed in recent years. Ralph feels quite unprepared for the conditions of the 1990s.

His department is in crisis through overspending. He knows it could result in the government disbanding the authority if the problem is not rectified. But there is fierce resistance to his plans for cutbacks and his colleagues are beginning to undermine him with alternative plans of their own. He feels his back is against the wall.

But he is mistrusted by his colleagues, because he keeps changing the 'hit list' of closures when he feels much resistance. They feel he doesn't have the courage of his convictions.

There are ways which promise solutions, but Ralph finds it hard to accept new ideas. He feels unable to shrug off the old municipal mentality and develop an enterprise outlook. Instead, he buries himself behind mountains of paperwork and blames everyone else – the members of the authority, the political forces behind them, the staff and the public. He is ready to retire.

Alan, the unemployed builder

Alan Sands is a young man who has set himself up in business as a building contractor with the help of The Prince's Youth Business Trust. He is now twenty-three and has spent much of his time since leaving school at sixteen working for building contractors. Prior to setting himself up in business, however, he had been unemployed for three years. He is confident that he has the skills to handle any domestic building job within reason and he has convinced The Prince's Youth Business Trust of this, too. On small jobs he works alone, but when necessary he employs the help of a labourer on a day-to-day basis. While his practical skills are well up to the tasks he has to carry out, his business skills, knowledge and appropriate attitudes are in their infancy. He is, however, keen to learn, and is making progress.

DISCUSSION POINTS

1. What personal opportunities do the changing economic circumstances offer you – this year? In five years' time?

2. What are your attitudes to profit, privatisation, welfare rights, job security and competition? Have your views changed over time?

3. How willing are you to take financial risks
   (a) affecting your own future?
   (b) affecting the future of friends, family or work mates?

SUMMARY

- we need to understand the changes that are taking place in the funding of provision of goods and services, and why.

- we need to recognise the needs and opportunities these bring.

- let us be prepared to adapt our attitudes and skills accordingly.

- realise that nobody takes risks for nothing.

- appreciate the advantages of the market system.

- think like an entrepreneur.

- be more prepared to survive or perish on our own merits.

- be more prepared to take risks and accept the consequences, whether good or bad.

- learn by our mistakes.

- be ready to play in the right league.

2
Who is Financial Information For?

Everyone, individuals and firms, uses financial information. It's the universal language in which all business activities are recorded, measured, controlled and communicated. Financial information is information about money. Its functions are:

- measuring performance

- recording value

- providing a medium of exchange in the market-place where organisations sell their goods and buy materials or factors of production like land and labour

- recording debts.

Only a tiny proportion of an organisation's finances will be in the form of money in the bank or in the cash box. Most will be in the form of 'money's worth' – assets which can be used to generate income – machines to make products to sell, property to generate rent, stocks to sell, and so on.

A self-employed builder may throw up his hands in horror at the thought of keeping any more than the most simple financial records. Tradesmen often hate paperwork and while they're doing it they're not laying bricks or mending cars. Their primary records are often jottings on cigarette packets. Equally the market trader may record market prices in his head while walking around the market prior to fixing those prices on his stalls.

But a large organisation couldn't rely on the thumb ruling, duck diving, hunch trusting, two-pocket banking horse-sense that a market trader may use to manage a business. Its income comes from too many sources and drains away from too many outlets for one

ISSUE OF £2,000,000,000

6% TREASURY STOCK 1999

INTEREST PAYABLE HALF-YEARLY ON 10 FEBRUARY AND 10 AUGUST FOR AUCTION ON 27 APRIL 1994

The above Stock is to be sold by auction on Wednesday 27th April 1994. Under the auction procedure applicants may bid for the stock and bids will be accepted in descending order of price.

Conditions

1. The principal and interest on the Stock will be a charge on the National Loans Fund, with recourse to the Consolidated Fund of the United Kingdom.

2. The Stock will be repaid at par on 10th August 1999.

3. [other conditions as to the issue of the Stock.]

BANK OF ENGLAND, LONDON. 19th April 1994.

APPLICATION FORM		
Amount applied for (in multiples of £1,000)	£	
Sum enclosed	£	
Signature(s)	Date	
Full name and address		

Cheques should be made payable to 'Bank of England' and crossed 'New Issues' and received not later than 10 a.m. on Wednesday 27th April 1994.

Fig. 2. How the Government borrows money. This is a simplified version of the kind of advertisement which the Government places in the financial press when it seeks to raise money to help cover the 'public sector borrowing requirement'. The bonds which are issued are nicknamed 'gilts', short for 'gilt-edged securities'.

WHERE YOUR TAXES GO

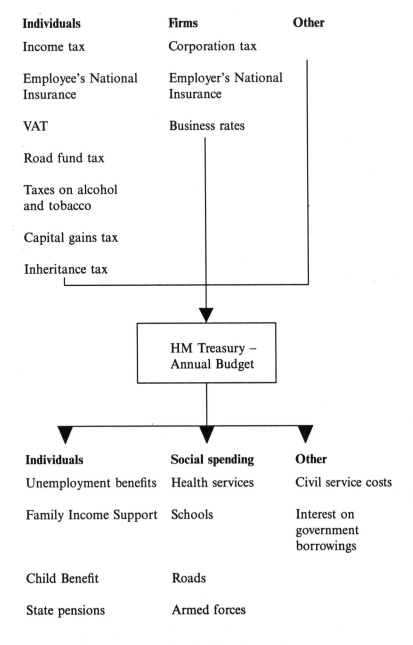

Fig. 3. Some of the things your taxes are spent on

person to keep a direct eye on them all. Its operations take place at many locations, often far out of reach of managers; money leaks from the system wherever there is inefficiency, wastage, poor judgement and even pilfering. In order to keep a grip on everything large amounts of data have to be collected on all aspects of activity wherever it takes place. It has to be analysed and interpreted before top managers get it, to filter it down to manageable proportions. The larger and more complex the firm's operations, the more pre-analysed and pre-interpreted it will have to be.

FINANCIAL INFORMATION IN THE PUBLIC SECTOR

While business funding comes from investment, borrowing and re-invested profits, Government funding comes from taxes, borrowing and profits from nationalised industries – notice the similarity?

The financial concerns of all organisations, public and private sector, are about the **sources and application of funds,** so let's have a look where each gets its funding from.

Raising money by taxes

Governments collect taxes in many ways; some taxes are **progressive** and some are **regressive**. When taxes are based directly on the money we earn, the higher earners shoulder most of the burden; after tax-free allowances, which we are all allowed, the high earners still have quite a lot of money left to tax, while very low earners' pay may not exceed the tax free allowance and so they pay nothing. This is why income tax is referred to as a progressve tax.

Multi-rate income tax bands make even greater demands on the high earners by increasing the proportion of income taxed as earnings rise.

Regressive taxes tax your money when you spend it and here low earners fare worst, because they have to spend all their money while high earners don't. VAT is a prime example of regressive tax.

Raising money by borrowing

The second way governments obtain their funding is through borrowing, mainly from the people. They do this by issuing bonds (IOUs) for a price which can be cashed in after a number of years. In the meantime interest is paid to the holders.

Raising money from nationalised industries

The third main way governments obtain their funding is from the profits of nationalised industries. These are companies in which the government holds at least fifty-one per cent of the shares and so is entitled to at least fifty-one per cent of the distributed profits (where they exist). Almost all the nationalised industries have now been re-privatised, however, and this source of funding is likely to die out completely before long.

Raising money for local government

Local government, ie county and town councils, obtain their funding from rates and taxes, like the **council tax** and the old **poll tax**, with a supplement from central government called the **rate support grant**.

Social costs

Both central and local governments have to balance income from all these sources with a very wide range of outgoings, but they also have an added complication that the private sector does not. They have to consider the **social costs** of projects. Social costs are not directly financial in nature. They include for example increased illness in the population as a result of the siting of a power station, increased noise because of a new road or increased truancy as a result of the closure of a local school and transference of pupils to one further away from their home. They do this by reducing all the costs to financial terms, eg the extra cash which would be needed by the Health Service to treat the estimated increase in illness, the cost of giving grants for double glazing to reduce noise nuisance, and the increased resources needed by the Education and/or Social Services Departments to combat the increase in truancy they think will result from the school closure.

The balance of payments surplus or deficit

Central government also has to consider the **balance of payments**, ie the difference between all funds coming into the country and all funds going out. Any shortfall has to be funded somehow, for example by borrowing from abroad or devaluing the currency. In recent years Japan has had by far the biggest balance of trade **surplus** each year. It has thereby become an immensely wealthy nation, and the yen has risen greatly in value. The United States and Britain have had the biggest balance of trade **deficits** in recent years. They have thereby fallen very heavily into debt, and the dollar and sterling have fallen heavily against other leading foreign currencies.

BUSINESS PEOPLE AND THE SELF-EMPLOYED

Businesses in the private sector are concerned with:

- making profits – who wants to risk their capital for nothing?

- keeping solvent – who wants to go bust?

- resisting hostile takeover bids – who wants to lose their job?

- growth of the business (some firms will deny this, but they wouldn't last long if it were true, for growth is a natural function of a healthy enterprise)

- keeping costs down and revenues up – who wants to lose money?

- setting prices at the optimum levels – who wants to lose customers? Then again, who wants to give anything away?

Investors are concerned mainly with their dividends and the value of their shares, and indirectly with profitability and future prospects. Dividends are usually paid out half-yearly (interim dividend at the half-year stage and final payment at the end of year). They amount to such a part of the profits (after taxation) as is decided by the directors. Not all the profit can be paid out each year – because it is very unlikely to all be in the form of cash.

Profit amounts to an increase in the net assets of a firm from one year to the next. If the firm is growing (as any healthy firm will be) then some of that increase will be in the form of non-cash assets: more stocks, more machinery and so on. Even that which is in cash is unlikely to be all paid out since some will be retained to provide working capital. If the directors hold back too much of it, though, the shareholders who employ them will be unhappy about it. There will be two reasons for this:

- They're being expected to risk even more of their money – the profit which is rightly theirs.

- The resale value of their shares will fall.

Predatory-natured companies will quickly spot share prices which drop below the value of the assets they represent and launch a takeover bid. They will buy enough shares to give them control, after which they will close the firm down. If the firm is one of its competitors there is an added bonus of getting rid of a competitor. Those companies will study share prices and company balance sheets. The former are published daily in newspapers like *The Financial Times* and more up-to-the-minute prices are available from stockbrokers. Balance sheets, from which information can be obtained regarding asset values, are published at least annually and are held on microfiches at Companies House (Cardiff and London). Many firms also produce interim reports at half-yearly or even quarterly intervals. The chairman and board of directors must strike a careful balance. They must keep the shareholders happy and keep share prices from falling below the asset values they represent on the one hand, but keep sufficient funds within the company to finance growth on the other. If you don't grow in the modern world you perish. Everyone else will grow.

One way the directors can make a profit retention less conspicuous is to transfer it from profit and loss account to a reserve account.

The chairman and board of directors of companies are interested in profitability, share prices and sources and application of funds. Consequently, they will handle such things as profit and loss accounts, interim accounts, balance sheets, budgets, stock market information, feasibility studies on new products, competing quotations, reports and plans for new investments and on how they are proposed to be financed.

LOCAL AUTHORITIES AND FINANCIAL INFORMATION

Local government is concerned to ensure that:

- There will be enough to pay for all the services planned. This will involve careful housekeeping at all levels and in all departments.

- The revenue from the public in rates and taxes is collected efficiently with acceptable control of arrears.

- Like all investors it will be concerned about the uncertainties of future costs when preparing the budgets for future years.

- That the planned expenditure of taxes does not place too great a financial burden on the citizens (especially those whom the party in power are relying on to re-elect them).

- The national debt (the amount the Government will have to pay back, with interest, to those people who have purchased Government bonds) is kept under control.

- Government departments have to take into account the social costs of projects.

NEWLY PRIVATISED INDUSTRIES AND FINANCIAL INFORMATION

As more and more state provision is edged into the private sector, a growing number of civil servants will have to radically change their attitude to funding and start using financial information in a very different way from what they have been used to. Privatisation has taken place in a number of ways.

- Privatisation of public utilities, ie selling of shares.

- Local Authority partnerships with the private sector.

- Contracting out.

- Sale of utilities to institutional investors.

- Sale of particular assets, eg British Rail hotels.

In public sector institutions performance control has tended to be by way of a number of committees – PESC (Public Expenditure Survey Committee), PAR (Programme Analysis and Review) and CPRS (Central Policy Review Staff) on the one hand and district and internal audit procedures on the other. Financial control was a case of assessing the amount of money needed to maintain the current levels of performance over the ensuing year. The reports of each institution would be scrutinised along with the others and committees would allocate funding for the following year. Since cuts would invariably be imposed in real terms it was worthwhile overestimating the costs.

The newly privatised industries will have to seek their funding from investors by offering a potentially good reward for risk. Since it will be private money involved, managers will have to take very great care in handling the finance efficiently, in order to keep their own jobs.

GRANT-MAINTAINED SCHOOLS AND NHS TRUSTS

Two services, the provision of which have long been taken for granted as the responsibility of the state, are education and health. But because of the need to tighten up efficiency of resource usage in these areas, they are being increasingly edged into the private sector. **Locally managed** schools and colleges will have to be more responsible for their own survival than they ever have had to before, ensuring that:

- there will be enough money to pay for services planned

- the school or college produces good value for money, measured in terms of outcomes (eg GCSE grades or truancy levels)

- enrolment numbers (and thus revenues) are kept high

- like other institutions, they will have to face uncertainties as to future costs and revenues

- good housekeeping is practised at all levels and in all departments, ie everybody sticks to their budgets and uses their funds wisely.

LOCALLY MANAGED HEALTH TRUSTS

Similarly, locally managed health trusts will have to ensure that:

- funding will be adequate to meet demand;

- any services provided outside of area, eg beds for patients resident in other counties, are paid for by those counties: in short, that the trusts do not stand the cost of providing services for which they do not receive funding;

- good value for money is achieved in finance usage, as measured by such things as waiting-lists; and that

- good housekeeping is achieved at all levels in all departments.

Uncertainty as to future costs (due to inflation) will concern local health trusts and grant-maintained schools and colleges when they are setting their budgets for subsequent years.

Gaining the expertise
Placing large amounts of money into the control of people not used to handling that level of finance, nor even managing their own financial affairs, poses a risk of wastage and abuse. So great is this risk that in August 1993 the Government's Audit Commission called for independent auditing of the accounts of grant-maintained schools, rather than relying on their own appointed auditors. Managers of such schools are going to have to cut their financial teeth rather quickly, therefore, if they are to maintain their independence of action, for if self-regulation doesn't work enforced regulation may follow. Sound skills of stewardship (financial record-keeping), financial control and investment appraisal will have to be learned. The same, of course, goes for managers of the new health trusts.

PYBT-SUPPORTED ENTREPRENEURS

Another category of newcomers to the market-place is going to have to handle financial information for, perhaps, the first time. These are the young unemployed who are being coaxed to begin standing on their own feet and creating a livelihood for themselves as entrepreneurs. Their sole income is to come from the profits on their activities and they will have to learn quickly how to keep their costs in check and match planned to actual performance. All candidates for help from The Prince's Youth Business Trust have to produce a business plan which is approved as feasible by a mentor/supervisor.

Getting used to financial responsibility
Like the new managers of health trusts and grant-maintained schools, the PYBT entrepreneurs will suddenly find themselves responsible for more money than they have ever handled before. Many will fall into the trap of spending it, failing to fully realise that it is not theirs to spend. Much (and in many cases most) of the income they receive from customers must go to pay their suppliers for providing the goods which they then sell on for a profit. Similarly, if they employ people in their business their wages must be paid before the PYBT employer takes anything for himself. Indeed, one PYBT youth entrepreneur told me:

'The trouble is I've never been used to having money, and now that I have it I just spend, spend, spend.'

Many tend to regard their income from sales or services as 'earnings'. Indeed, they often actually call it that, and so treat it as their own money, to do what they want with. But it's only the net profit, *after everything else has been paid* (suppliers' accounts, wages, bills, etc) and provisions for repairs and so on have been set aside, that is theirs as actual earnings. And the earnings can't be reckoned without proper book-keeping and financial control methods.

The PYBT try to help them develop this awareness by making it a condition of the grants that they complete and submit a reasonably detailed report to show the quality of their record-keeping and financial control each month.

The grants they receive to buy fixed assets are paid direct to the suppliers. This prevents them getting carried away by the sudden presence of large sums of money in their hands and using it instead to relieve pent-up spending desires.

CASE STUDIES: INFORMATION IN ACTION

How Theresa follows through

Theresa L'Pralm sees her role as that of taking decisions. She knows that successful decision making requires access to the right information, of the right level of complexity and at the right time. But, making the decision is not enough, you have to make things work out in practice. So she is concerned to ensure that her costs and revenues conform to the planned (budgeted) figures.

Ralph needs to win support

Although Ralph Elmaster is the General Manager of the District Health Authority, he is accountable to the committee made up of District and County Councillors and members of the medical profession. He has to keep them informed of his authority's performance and also win their support for his plans. Most of the committee members directly represent the public, so if the public are not happy nor will they be. Ralph would be well advised to pay attention to public relations matters, but he doesn't. Nor does he even do a proper job of informing his staff of what is going on and why.

The DHA (District Health Authority) obtains its funding from the RHA (Regional Health Authority) who, in turn, obtain it from the government. All DHAs have to compete for funds from their regional authority. The latter will also need to be regularly informed of how the funds are used.

The National Audit Office takes a keen interest in the financial affairs of all such authorities. It needs to be satisfied that 'principles of best practice' have been followed, that they have been receiving good value for money spent and that there are no irregularities in accounting procedures.

Alan: 'Paperwork's just a waste of time.'

Alan Sands has had no business training to speak of. Like many newly self-employed people, he tends to feel that time spent keeping records is time when he could be earning money. His wife started to keep his books, but she had no training either, and soon gave up. As a PYBT-assisted person, Alan has to submit monthly financial reports on his business performance and his cash flow. The reports are simple and straightforward providing you have the information. As Alan's record-keeping falls more and more into arrears, though, his information will become harder and harder to recover and, invariably, some will be lost for good.

DISCUSSION POINTS

1. What financial information do you encounter at work and why?

2. Could you do a better job with more information and, if so, what type?

3. Why would shareholders want to read the financial press?

SUMMARY

- Business managers need financial information to enable them to control costs and revenues, make profits and invest for the future.

- Lenders want to see evidence that firms will be able to pay their debts now and in the future. They want to know how much of the owners' or shareholders' money there is to match that supplied by lenders.

- Shareholders read share prices and business articles in financial papers, as well as stockbrokers' bulletins and companies' annual reports.

- Governments must know how much money they need to raise,

how much to finance by taxation and how to distribute the tax burden.

- Those involved in Government expenditure descisions will need information on the hidden, social costs as well as the directly financial ones.

- Governments need to balance imports with exports, or face extra borrowing and currency devaluation.

- Auditors want to satisfy themselves that records have been kept properly and that they show a 'true and fair view' of the organisation's affairs.

3
Speaking the Language of Finance

RECORDING DAILY BUSINESS TRANSACTIONS

The functions of accounting can be simply stated:

- recording what happened

- reporting

- interpreting

- predicting what is likely to happen

- controlling what is happening.

All these functions focus on two things:

- the circulation of funds in a firm

- the financial structure of the firm.

Everyday transactions
Daily financial transactions include sales (and goods received back), purchases (and goods sent back), services provided to customers for a fee by the organisation, services provided to the firm for a fee, payments received from customers, and payments made to suppliers, employees and anyone else to whom the firm has a financial obligation.

Using standard accounts records books
The day books
The initial record of sales (and sales returns) and purchases (and

purchase returns) is made in four **day books** designed for the purpose, eg the **sales day book**. They include a separate column for each rate of VAT and analysis columns for each different kind of purchase or sale – useful for transferring them to the less detailed, cumulative record known as the **ledger** (see below). This might only be entered up once a month and such writing up is known as **posting**. For book-keeping purposes services provided to customers for a fee are regarded as sales.

The cash book
The payments received from customers and payments made to suppliers, employees and so on, are entered in a simple book known as the **cash book**.

The petty cash book
Small, but frequent, cash transactions, such as reimbursements of employees' expenses are recorded in the **petty cash book**. A system of topping the fund up periodically to a set level is usually employed and this is called the **imprest** system. The level is known as the **imprest amount**. A petty cash book is an 'analysed' version of the cash book. It permits analysis of the type of expenditure so that monthly totals can be found before posting to the ledger. Without it the ledger would become cluttered with small amounts.

The petty cashier is entrusted with a float (say £50); at all times he or she must have in the cash-box that value in money, vouchers for cash paid out and receipts (money + vouchers + receipts equals imprest amount). Every now and again he will exchange the receipts for a cash top-up from the main cashier. When the petty cashier pays out any money to an employee (perhaps to buy a small stationery item which the firm has run out of) the employee must sign a petty cash voucher and this is put in the tin in place of the cash. When the employee brings back a receipt the voucher should be destroyed, otherwise the cash + vouchers + receipts will not equal the imprest amount. It's surprising how many firms do not do this. It's a simple and effective system, if adhered to, but many firms have an obsession about keeping every scrap of paper.

The ledger
The ledger accounts are in **double-entry** form. Goods purchased by customers are posted on the left of their ledger, and payments received for them posted on the right. The reverse is the case for goods purchased by the firm from suppliers. This way there will be a

balance of entries on the left or right depending on whether the account holder is in debt or credit to the firm.

All transactions have a dual nature. In other words when a customer pays his bill his account must be **credited** and the cashier or bank who received the cheque must be **debited**. At the end of each month the debit balances should equal the credit balances. This exercise is called striking a **trial balance**.

For a full treatment of double-entry book-keeping please refer to *How to Master Book-Keeping* in this series.

The journal

Sometimes transactions are made where no money changes hands. For example a swap or partial swap is made (part-exchange), or a customer's debt is written off because he is declared bankrupt. Just because no money changes hands doesn't mean the transaction doesn't have to be recorded. The book for recording it is the journal, quite a simple book to enter.

The postage book

Quite large amounts of cash may be spent on postage stamps. These transactions have to be recorded, along with the usage of the stamps, in order to keep track of where they're going. A simple postage book is used for this, and it has a similar format to the petty cash book. It shows stamps in hand on the left, and stamps used on the right. It's another 'imprest' system; when necessary a further payment is made to the postage clerk by the cashier, so the clerk can buy stamps to top up the imprest system. This job is often carried out by a firm's receptionist. Large firms will use a franking machine instead.

Stock records

The stores represent a potentially fast-flowing leak from a firm's resources, in the form of pilfering. Surprisingly, however, relatively little attention is often paid to recording of ingoings and outgoings here. Strict stock recording tends to be more likely where high-cost durables are concerned, like electrical appliances. It's a simple matter – just recording each item in (with serial number if relevant) and each item out.

Transactions and their destinations

Type of transaction	Where recorded
Purchases	– Purchase day book
Purchase returns	– Purchase returns day book
Sales (and services)	– Sales day book
Sales returns	– Sales returns day book
Cash and banking	– Cash book
Small cash transactions	– Petty cash book
Non-cash adjustments	– Journal
Postage	– Postage book
Stock movement	– Stock book
Wages	– Wages book
Monthly accumulations of transactions	– Ledger divisions

Although these are called 'books' they don't have to be in book form. They can be 'Kalamazoo' type sheets, cards or in spreadsheet, or other computerised accounting formats.

These 'books' serve as the initial entry from which the monthly entries into the ledger are made and are, thus, called **books of prime entry**. Occasionally you'll find this stage bypassed and entries made directly into the ledger. This is called the **slip system**. It is used where accounts have to be kept very up to date, such as in banking, and wherever automated accounting systems are used. Where postings are made directly to the ledger from invoice copies those copies are filed to form the equivalent of the day book. This I call the 'slip + 1' system, because an extra invoice copy is needed.

In the accounts of some smaller firms, such as self-employed people, the ledgers, too, are sometimes dispensed with. Instead, the invoices (copies, in the case of invoices sent out) are merely filed together with other unpaid ones for each customer or supplier in date order. This takes the place of the personal ledger (sales and purchase). As soon as each is paid it's stamped and removed to be filed with all the paid ones. This version I call the 'slip + 2' system because two additional copies of each invoice are needed.

For version 'slip + 1' a firm's invoices really need to be printed in triplicate; for version 'slip + 2' they need to be in quadruplicate.

DIVIDING THE JOBS BETWEEN SPECIALISTS

In a small firm the same person will do the recording of all kinds of transactions. It's not surprising, therefore, that you'll find short cuts taken. That person will often be the proprietor and he or she may have neither the knowledge nor the inclination or time to learn the professional methods of book-keeping.

However, as the firm grows, the larger number of daily transactions will eventually mean taking on office staff, and sooner or later the book-keeping task will be divided up. Consequently, the firm will then employ people specially for ledger work, others for day-book work, and a specialised cashier. At this level, professional orthodox accounting techniques are almost certain to be used.

Repetition leads to perfection, and clerks who specialise in one task are more likely to learn from experience. For example they will learn that a discrepancy which is divisible by nine is likely to be due to two digits being written the wrong way round, eg 45 for 54, and other 'tricks of the trade'. When employees are specialised they'll be able to get through more transactions between them than if not.

KEEPING INFORMATION UP TO DATE

Day books should be entered daily wherever possible, though in the smallest of firms this is sometimes not feasible. In fact, they are sometimes not kept at all. In such cases it's essential that all invoices are numbered on receipt to avoid losing any. If day books are kept they usually tend to be totalled and cross-cast at the end of each page. They are then entered ('posted') into the ledger at least once a month.

The ledgers are **balanced** each month. This is essential, since the firm must control the time it's taking for its customers to pay their accounts, so that it can pay its own suppliers on time. If this isn't done the firm is likely to find it's paying its bills more quickly, on the average, than its customers are settling their accounts. This will lead to it running out of cash even if it's making high and profitable sales. Cash flow is more important than anything else.

There are, as already mentioned, cases where ledgers have to be kept very up to date indeed, as in banking. There, ledger posting will be done by computer within hours, or minutes of every transaction.

GAINING ECONOMIES THROUGH CENTRALISATION

As pointed out in Chapter 1, increased world competition means all firms are now under pressure to reduce their costs to a minimum, and so tend towards 'the perfectly efficient firm'. We also know that specialisation leads to efficiency, because repetition breeds speed, and specialists are more likely to learn by their experience.

The move to control by head offices

Many national firms with branches in various towns (shops and warehouses, for example), because of centralised buying practices, may only have enough daily transactions to employ a single book-keeper in each branch. Consequently, that all-rounder will not have the advantage of specialisation. Different factory sites will be another example. Here they may produce much but have few transactions to record, as all produce is sold through outlets elsewhere. Nor may such branches be able to justify computerised accounting systems; even if they can afford the hardware, they may not be able to justify the specialised training for staff. Many multi-branch firms are now finding they are being forced to cut overheads by going over to centralised accounting. This means that while daily records are often kept in a day book at the branch, a copy of this is sent each day to head office for ledger posting by specialists, with the aid of powerful computers. Alternatively, they might enter the initial data into a computer terminal at the branch linked directly to the firm's central computer.

The need to trim fixed costs

Another motive for such cost-cutting is that costs of administrative staff are *fixed* costs. They have to be paid whatever the level of sales, unlike production worker costs, or salesmen's commissions, which don't. In these increasingly uncertain times firms are keen to reduce their fixed costs to a minimum, to make their profitability more predictable.

Furthermore, administrative costs in the UK have been rising way out of proportion to other costs of production. In the 1950s they amounted to about twenty per cent of total costs, but by the mid-1980s they were more than fifty per cent. It's not surprising that firms have to find a suitable way of reducing them. Furthermore, administrative staff cost more than just their wages to keep – sometimes they're on inflation-proof pension schemes and continue to receive salary during periods of sickness.

The penalty of falling profits

The meaning of high profits is not just to fill the pockets of the owners. Without profits shareholders will sell their shares as sure as morning follows night, for there's no market which operates more aggressively and competitively than the stock market. And if they all sell their shares, share prices will go down, and when they dip below the value of the assets they represent another firm may well step in, buy them up and sell off the firm in bits. If this happens it may not be just *some* employees who will lose their jobs, but *all* of them – that's the reality.

UNDERSTANDING THE STANDARD FORMATS

There are standard ways of recording particular kinds of financial information. Some of these **accounting conventions** have been in force for a very long time. 'Double-entry book-keeping', for example, is known to date back to 1304, and perhaps it was around even before that.

Some of the old conventions seem superfluous to us today and have, in the past few decades, been avoided – the use of words like 'per' and 'pro' and 'by' in the ledgers, for example. However, some staff still persist in these old so-called 'proper' ways.

But just as some conventions are disappearing others are being added, and some of these have a compulsory nature about them, enforced by law. HM Customs & Excise, for example, requires certain information to be recorded in an acceptable way. Similarly, the Registrar of Companies compels limited companies to use certain specified formats for published annual accounts.

As well as the mandatory formats that have been added to accounting practice there is also persuasive pressure to abide by others. The **Accounting Standards Committee**, made up of members of all the main accounting associations, produces **Statements of Standard Accounting Practice (SSAPs)** for use in allowing for inflation in accounts.

On a more detailed level there are also conventions about recording individual transactions, and about the formats used in financial management, such as cash flow projections, break-even analysis and statements of contributions to overheads, which are used to prevent a firm ceasing production prematurely.

Why standard formats are necessary

Why are these standard formats necessary? There are a number of reasons. Speed and ease of comprehension are among them. All users of financial information in the modern world need to be able to extract the information they require quickly and easily. Standardisation of formats helps this. It makes it feasible to learn the formats in which particular kinds of information are recorded whatever the firm, so you can locate and comprehend the particular information you're interested in with minimum difficulty.

Communicating easily
Communication is a crucial aspect of efficient business performance and communication failure a major problem. Standardisation of accounting formats and language reduces the chance of this. Without it record-keeping would be like writing letters in languages you made up as you went along. Only the writer could read and understand them and even he may fail to do so.

Comparing like with like
Comparability is another reason. Accounting is a science and the usefulness of scientific information is partly determined by its comparability. It's difficult to decide, for investment purposes, between companies who are using different depreciation policies and different allowances for inflation, for example. The more similar the formats the more comparable the data, whether comparing between firms, or between different trading periods in the same firm. Secondly, for the capital market to work efficiently, buyers and sellers of shares must have as much information as possible, and the more clear and easy to compare with others it is the more they will comprehend it and be able to use it effectively.

Combating 'creative accounting'
The danger of being misled by 'creative accounting' is another reason for promoting standard formats. What is unsaid can be as significant as what is said in accounts and creative accounting can make a bad situation look good. It can also make a profitable result look less so; tax minimisation is more important than share prices for small firms and the self-employed.

Minimising tax avoidance
HM Inland Revenue and HM Customs & Excise will be concerned to minimise 'tax avoidance' (however innocent or otherwise) by omission of some sources of income or some transactions from the records. By compelling people to keep records with the prescribed minimum level of detail of all sales and purchase transactions it's less likely that some will escape the tax net.

Protection from embezzlement
Embezzlement is always a risk when owners are employing staff to handle their assets. Indeed, this was the reason for introducing marbling on the page edges of ledgers. Should a page be taken out it will be noticed.

Marketability of skills
Universality of skill and knowledge applications makes it possible
for someone who has worked in accounts in one firm to get a similar
job in another. It's essential for the factor market to work efficiently
that the financial knowledge and skills of workers can be applied to
the needs of all firms. If some firms had their peculiar ways of
keeping financial records their existing staff alone would have the
relevant knowledge and skills. They would not be subject to
competition, and so their wages would creep above the true market
value of the staff they related to. This would erode the firm's
competitiveness, profits would fall, share prices would decrease and
a takeover might well follow.

Teachability
Standardisation makes accountancy teaching possible, and also the
testing of outcomes by accountancy examinations. It's easier to
measure quality of performance of financial activity where there are
benchmarks for good work.

SOME COMMON MISCONCEPTIONS ABOUT ACCOUNTS

Sales are earnings – no.
Most of the money from sales has to go to paying suppliers and
overheads. Only the final residue of profit after everything else has
been paid out is earnings.

Capital employed and working capital are the same thing – no.
Capital employed is the net assets, ie the fixed assets including
buildings, machines and vehicles plus the current assets including
stock debtors and cash minus the current liabilities, ie what has to
be paid out within the year. Working capital is merely the difference
between the current assets and current liabilities; it does not include
things like buildings, machines and vehicles.

*Debits in the cash account is money paid out and credits is money
received – no.*
It's the other way round. The common misconception comes from
the fact that it appears that way on your bank statements, but they
are representations of the bank's books, not yours. Money paid into
the bank puts you in the bank's credit from *its* point of view, but
from your point of view it puts the bank in your debit. The bank
accounts from its points of view, while you account from yours.

All discounts should be entered in the books – no.
Only early settlement discounts should be entered.

The balance sheet is named so because it balances – no.
It's called the balance sheet because it's a list of the residual balances in the ledger after the annual revenue accounts have been compiled.

You don't account for things like electricity usage until you receive the bill – wrong.
At the end of the year an estimate has to be made for things like electricity used but as yet unbilled. Similarly, in the next year's accounts that estimated figure has to be deducted from the accounts to allow for electricity billed in that year but used in the previous year.

Goodwill should always be shown as it is an asset of the business – no.
It is only appropriate to show goodwill in the accounts where an amalgamation or business transfer is taking · place. Once the transaction is complete goodwill should be written off.

All expenses, including wining and dining, are reclaimable against tax – wrong.
Only in special circumstances can you now reclaim tax on things like wining and dining.

It's better to sell less at a high price than more at a low one – not necessarily so.
Turning your stock over twice at forty per cent profit would, on the face of it, be preferable to turning it over once at fifty per cent profit in the same period, though you must take into account any extra direct selling costs like salesmen's commissions or delivery costs.

CASE STUDIES: TALKING FINANCE

Theresa in control

Theresa L'Pralm is just as conversant with all the accounting procedures in the firm as the book-keeping clerks who carry them out, after all she started her career in the accounts office. But she doesn't even see accounts now, she just sees the interim accounting reports that are produced. A characteristic of intelligent, goal-orientated behaviour is selecting out the information that is relevant from that which is not.

Alan gets behind

Like many sole proprietors, Alan Sands has had the attitude:

'While I'm keeping books I'm not earning money. It's a problem that can be put aside for the moment. I'll just store up my papers and have a blitz on it later.'

But under the terms of Alan's PYBT support, he must send in monthly reports on his performance and his cash flow. Now, five months behind, PYBT has demanded that he do so.

He is now learning the bitter lesson that records are very hard to complete long after the event. Things always get lost, details are found missing from cheque stubs and explanations of transactions are forgotten. What is known as 'incomplete records accounting' can be a nightmare (see *How to Master Book-Keeping*, by Peter Marshall, How To Books, pp156-165).

DISCUSSION POINTS

1. How conventional are the record-keeping techniques you use, or have used, at work?

2. Does your firm's petty cash system, or that of a previous employer, work well? If not, why?

3. Do you know a firm whose stock control leaves much to be desired? If so, how would you deal with the problem?

SUMMARY

- The book-keepers record the circulation of funds and the financial structure of the firm.

- Initial entries are made in day books and monthly totals posted to the ledger, but slip systems are sometimes used, which avoid one or both of these.

- It's easy to control petty cash on an imprest system, because the cash-box should always contain the imprest amount (cash + petty cash vouchers + receipts).

- Because there are two sides to every transaction (a debit one and a credit one), at the end of the month the total debits will equal the total credits if these have been entered correctly.

● Good stock control can save the firm money.

● 'Books' don't have to actually be books: they can be looseleaf, or computerised.

● Specialisation among accounting staff can lead to economies and greater expertise.

● Keeping the books up to date enables them to be used for control purposes and prevents information loss.

● There are conventional accounting formats, some of which are required by law.

● Standardisation in record-keeping methods is important for reasons of ease of comprehension, comparability, avoidance of misleading information, marketability of accounting staff's skills and teachability of the subject.

4
Understanding Financial Reports

THE DIFFERENCE BETWEEN REPORTS AND RECORDS

In essence:

- records deal with data
- reports deal with information.

The essence of reports is to present information selected for a purpose, rather than simply logging everything, as records do. Data and information are two different things. Data (plural of datum) are facts, while information is those facts plus interpretation. This interpretation may involve applying analytical and interpretive rules, combined with knowledge, experience and common sense. Consequently, reporting tends to be done by more senior and experienced staff than recording.

Top management's job is to make decisions, not to compute figures. They will have neither the time, nor necessarily the skills, to do so. What makes a good accountant is different from what makes a good manager. Top managers' strengths are their ability to deal with uncertainty and take risks. Accountants, in contrast, are trained to avoid risks. Their motto is, in fact, 'caution is the greatest of all virtues'. It is better that people trained in careful analysis should interpret whatever data that lends itself to reliable and valid interpretation, and then present it to management to take it from there. Their job is handling the uncertainties. Horses for courses, as they say.

Management reporting
This kind of reporting is a routine activity in organisations. The main features are:

- most reports present a collation of facts

- they offer alternative answers to a problem
- they have a conclusion
- they offer recommendations.

Another kind of reporting is for monitoring purposes – keeping actual performance in line with that which has been planned. Again, it would just cloud the issue to be given details of each and every sale, purchase or expense transaction. Budgets (plans) will have been made in terms of daily, weekly, half-yearly and yearly figures. Consequently totals of actual figures for those same periods are needed for monitoring purposes. These can be compiled from the records and submitted to management. There isn't the level of interpretation here that goes into reports like **feasibility studies** for investment decisions, but it does involve selecting from the records that which is relevant to the purpose.

All functional departments have to report their performance to senior management for general control purposes. Lots of different kinds of information may be involved – periodic sales, costs of production and overhead expenses, to name but a few. Reports on trading figures, and VAT collected and paid on them, have to be sent to HM Customs & Excise. There are standard forms for this. The firms act as unpaid collectors of VAT for HM Customs & Excise, deducting what VAT they, themselves, have had to pay on goods and services, before remitting the balance to HM Customs & Excise.

Directors' reports
At the top of the management tree, too, the directors of companies have to report on the company's performance:

- to shareholders – revenue accounts and balance sheet

- to the Inland Revenue – revenue accounts and balance sheet

- to the public – by filing a copy of the published annual accounts and directors' reports at Companies House. (There is a different report for publication purposes to that for internal purposes.)

Annual reports to shareholders
Under the provisions of the Companies Acts, directors must make an annual report to shareholders and it must be accompanied by:

1. a profit and loss account which shows details of income and expenditure
2. a balance sheet, which shows
   - the value of all assets, fixed and current
   - the amount of all categories of current liabilities
   - long-term liabilities
   - share capital and reserves
   - provision for taxation and loan repayments.

These reports must give a 'true and fair' view of the financial affairs of the company. They must also include:

- details of any unusual financial facts
- the effects of any changes in accounting procedures
- comments by the directors and auditors on the accounts.

The annual report must also disclose such things as the value of exports, directors' salaries which exceed £60,000 a year, and donations to political parties and/or charities.

The auditors' report
The auditors' report should state the methods used for valuing stock and other assets, including the way depreciation figures have been worked out. This report will probably be the most detailed of all in the annual submission to shareholders.

Government department reports
Just as private companies have to report each year to their financiers – the shareholders – so, too, do Government departments have to report annually to their direct funding body, the Treasury. Each year departments must present reports which will include an estimate of the funding required to maintain activity through the next year. As funding requests are invariably slashed by the parliamentary expenditure sub-committee concerned, there is an incentive to overestimate costs.

Other reports
At the other end of the scale, the young self-employed, being nurtured to stand on their own feet by organisations like The Prince's Youth Business Trust are also obliged to make regular reports to their backers. Each month a report on their business performance and their cash flow has to be submitted.

Corporate image

A firm's image, the way it is seen by the outside world, is significantly influenced by its reporting. Regular and accurate reporting gives an impression of openness, which breeds confidence in the integrity of the people involved. Openness reduces the likelihood of corruption. To quote the economist Jeremy Bentham:

'Sunlight is the greatest of all disinfectants, publicity the most efficient policeman.'

WHAT HAS TO BE REPORTED?

The different kinds of things that have to be reported are too numerous to list, but the key thing in both private companies and Government departments is the annual report.

Private company accounts

In private companies this comprises the **revenue accounts** and **balance sheet** (plus accompanying directors' and auditors' reports, mentioned in the last section). The revenue accounts incorporate the **manufacturing account** and/or the **trading account**, the **profit and loss account** and the **appropriation account**.

The manufacturing account
The manufacturing account shows the costs of production, including opening and closing stocks of raw materials, purchases throughout the year, direct factory costs, including labour, apportioned power, rent and administrative costs.

The trading account
The trading account sets out opening and closing stocks, purchases and carriage inwards costs, together with any direct labour costs of selling, like salesmen's commissions. It also shows the sales revenue. The profit and loss account gives details of all overhead expenses, and also income from non-trading sources, like rents or investments in shares of other companies, or interest received.

The appropriation account
The appropriation account shows how the net profit has been allocated – so much to taxation, so much to reserve account for financing growth, so much to shareholders, for example.

The balance sheet

The balance sheet shows the state of affairs of a firm at the end of a trading period. It sums up the assets and liabilities, and shows how the balance between them is matched by the capital account.

The balance sheet shows the value of fixed assets, including land and buildings, fixtures and fittings, machinery and vehicles, together with allowances for depreciation. It will show the current assets, including cash at bank and cash in hand, stock and debtors, together with an appropriate allowance for some of the latter becoming uncollectable. It will show what it is owed in the short term, and what it owes out to trade creditors and on bank overdrafts, as well as expenses which have been incurred but not yet billed and, conversely, expenses which have been paid for but not yet used. The long-term liabilities of the firm will be reported in this document. These include long-term loans, and the capital of the firm which is owed, in the final event, back to the owners who put it up in the first place.

EXPLAINING FINANCIAL DISCREPANCIES

Sometimes reports have to be made to explain discrepancies. A few examples are as follows:

- when the bank statement doesn't tally with the cash book – **bank reconciliation statement**.

- high profits and low bank balance, or vice versa – the **statement of sources and application of funds**.

- where there is a crisis of solvency even though high profits have been made and there is money in the bank – **the statement of working capital flow**.

KNOWING HOW OFTEN TO REPORT

Annual reports

There's a deadline for submitting annual accounts to Companies House, and companies can be fined for missing it. A company's official year ends on 31 March, but it may choose to end its trading year at some other date. An auditors' report and a directors' report have to be submitted along with the final accounts to shareholders, to Companies House and to HM Inland Revenue. These reports are prepared *after* the final accounts, as they are based upon them.

ARMSTRONG ENGINEERING LTD
TRADING, PROFIT & LOSS ACCOUNT
For year ended 31 December 19X1

Turnover	308,000
Cost of Sales	177,000
Gross profit	131,000
Administration expenses	54,500
	76,500
Interest payable	900
Profit on ordinary activities before taxation	75,600
Tax on profit from ordinary activities	32,000
Profit on ordinary activities after taxation	43,600
Profit and loss account balance	
Undistributed profits b/f from last year	23,400
	67,000
Proposed dividends	34,500
Undistributed profits c/f to next year	32,500

BALANCE SHEET
as at 31 December 19X1

	Cost	Less Provision for Depreciation	Net Book
Fixed assets			
Premises	103,400		103,400
Fixtures and Fittings	10,000	500	9,500
Machinery	40,000	2,000	38,000
Motor Van	10,000	2,000	8,000
	163,400	4,500	158,900
Current assets			
Stock	18,000		
Debtors	48,700		
Cash at Bank	19,850		
Cash in Hand	50		
		86,600	
Less Creditors			
Amounts falling due within 1 yr	22,500		
Accruals	4,000		
Proposed Dividends	34,500	61,000	25,600
Total Net Assets			184,500
Provision for Liabilities and Charges			
Taxation			32,000
Shareholders Funds			
Authorised Share capital			
100,000 Preference Shares of £1	100,000		
100,000 Ordinary Shares of £1	100,000		
	200,000		
Issued Share Capital			
30,000 Preference Shares of £1		30,000	
90,000 Ordinary Shares of £1		90,000	
		120,000	
Capital and Reserves			
Profit & Loss Account balance		32,500	152,500
			184,500

Fig. 4 Example of final accounts.

Interim reports

Interim accounts may be compiled half-yearly, quarterly or even monthly for internal control purposes, depending on company policy. Managers and directors need interim accounts to compare actual performance with planned performance, so that they can take remedial action if necessary. It's important for the company, and for those managing it, that they're seen to be able to achieve the targets they set and the performance they promise to their shareholders.

Daily or weekly sales reports are self-explanatory in terms of frequency. Stock-take periods vary from firm to firm, but will be at least once a year; often an independent stock-taking firm will be employed for the purpose.

It's not very likely that the cash book will balance with the bank statement at the end of any month, because the bank and the firm will have different information. Therefore, the bank reconciliation statement will have to be done at the end of each month.

VAT reports are submitted monthly or quarterly, depending on whichever the business elects to do. In practice, most submit them quarterly.

Reports of financial feasibility of projects, and other reports on specific matters (damage reports, for example) will be done as and when required.

UNDERSTANDING HOW TO WRITE REPORTS

Reporting may simply involve giving various details of functional performance, eg costs and revenues, daily sales figures or motor expenses. On the other hand, they may be much more technical. They may be interpretations and reformulations of 'raw data' from an audit, rehashed to make it more comprehensible to the recipient, cutting out the irrelevant detail and presenting only the facts pertinent to decision-making or some other purpose. Such facts will also be presented in the most easily assimilable way and will often include recommendations.

Some have to be in a standard format, eg the annual accounts of limited companies. (Here there are four alternatives allowed by law for the balance sheet and six for the profit and loss account.)

Some will even have to be made on pre-printed forms. These may be designed to keep things simple. VAT forms, for example, tell the user exactly what sorts of information to put where. Unfortunately, however, not all standard report forms are as user-friendly.

Those which do not require a standard format should still follow the conventional rules of report writing, that is, they should include facts, and interpretations of facts, but not normally opinions. Where relevant, they should state alternative approaches to resolving any problem which the report is about and include a conclusion and recommendations. The format of the directors' annual report to shareholders is not fixed, but there are mandatory comments (see page 60).

Non-limited firms are not restricted in the formats of their final accounts. However, they still follow conventional format styles in the interests of comparability and other reasons outlined on pages 53-54.

- **Statements of sources and application of funds** tend to follow a common format. This provides an analysis of any increases in capital or liabilities, and decreases in assets. This is followed by any changes of the reverse nature, ie decreases in capital or liabilities and increases in assets. The balance is then explained in terms of increased or decreased cash.

- A **working capital flow statement** is laid out in the same way, except that parts one and two include only changes in things which are not included in the calculation of working capital. The balance is explained in terms of analysis of changes in working capital rather than changes in cash, as in the sources and application of funds statement.

The Prince's Youth Business Trust

The Prince's Youth Business Trust makes loans and bursaries to young people to set them up in business. It requires them to complete a monthly progress report, with the help of their appointed adviser. The information must show how actual sales compare with forecasted sales, how much stock is held, the number of orders outstanding, how actual costs compare with forecasted costs, whether there are any problems with bad debts and whether income has been covering costs.

On the reverse of the form is a cash flow report. This asks for a comparison between forecasted and actual cash flow figures for the previous month and for the year to date. The details include receipts from sales and other sources, cash paid for trading expenses, cash paid for capital items, loan repayments, VAT and cash taken as drawings. Lastly, it asks for the closing bank balance.

The report form also requires details of how much money is owed in and out of the business, and how much needs to be put aside for replacement of assets.

Accounting conventions

There are accounting conventions on the way reports of certain kinds of information should be made, the SSAPs on inflation accounting, for example.

The order of the reporting process is:

- collection of data

- recording of data

- analysis of data

- reporting.

Many reports can be turned out automatically, or almost so, from data held on a firm's computer. Information flow determines the sensitivity to change in an organisation. Frequent, full, up-to-date and accurate reporting is therefore necessary. In many large, modern firms functional data is provided by managers to a data processing department. It can then be analysed and returned as useful feedback on performance, enabling managers to take remedial action where necessary.

Management information

Managers need information for:

- Planning, implementing, controlling and reviewing.

- Co-ordinating the affairs of different departments.

- Keeping investors and lenders fully informed so that they can make sound judgements about the firm. They may for example wish to compare one year with another in the same firm, or that firm with another in the same year.

- Showing investors and other interested parties like trade unions where the profits have gone and how retained profits are being used.

- Assuring investors that the firm is using their money efficiently.

- Assuring sponsors, like PYBT, that grants are being used for the purpose for which they were given.

REPORTS REQUIRED BY LAW

Firms' legal reporting obligations include:
- Presenting published accounts and directors' and auditors' reports of limited companies.
- Reporting to HM Customs & Excise on the amounts of VAT revenue collected on its behalf by the business.
- Satisfying HM Inland Revenue that all relevant information has been disclosed so that the right tax bill can be computed.

CASE STUDIES: FINANCIAL REPORTS

Theresa: 'Report to me'

Theresa L'Pralm is too busy, and her span of attention is too wide, to deal with fine detail. She requires the information she receives from the various departments of the firm to be in analysed, and pre-interpreted form.

There are two aspects of decision behaviour – 'decision-making' and 'decision-taking'. She can't do them both when there are only 24 hours in a day and only so much room in her head. 'Decision-making' involves collecting the data, recording it, analysing it and interpreting it. She would never actually get around to deciding between alternatives if she did all this 'decision-making' work herself. Her role is to 'take' (not 'make') the decisions. She expects the alternatives to be presented to her in easily comprehensible form, backed up with the supporting arguments and evidence, and in only as much detail as is necessary. The compilation of these reports does not involve risk and so can be done by others; her job is to handle the risks so she must choose between the alternatives rather than set them up in the first place – 'Horses for courses' and there could hardly be a more appropriate metaphor for the difference between these roles.

Ralph's 'snow job' backfires

Ralph Elmaster feels he is up against a brick wall. He has to make cutbacks, but the members of the District Authority are resisting all his attempts to do so. He is exasperated by the fact that they cannot see the sense and necessity of his plans.

But has he given them enough information? 'Yes', he says. But perhaps he's given them too much – 'data' that is. They are all busy people; they include members of the medical profession, who have little time to spare and are snowed under with their own paperwork. They do not have time to wade through the mountains of facts and figures he gives them, so the result is most of it doesn't get read at all. If he paid more attention to presentation and less to volume, giving them better analysed, better interpreted, more concise information – 'more wheat and less chaff' – they would be able to digest it without threatening their own busy schedules. Ralph argues that the problems are complex and so all this detail is necessary. 'The members expect it', he says. But he is just projecting his own state of mind on to them – they neither want, nor need, to hide behind heaps of paper.

Most of the DHA members are District or County Councillors and so represent the public. So if Ralph can't sell his ideas to them – can't at least half convince them of the necessity for his cutbacks – he'll never get the members on his side. And he can only hope to get the public's support if he tells them why it's necessary, and what the plus side of the reorganisation is. They will undoubtedly continue to grumble, but they are more likely to accept the bitter medicine if they know why it's necessary. But Ralph has hardly given that a thought. He has the mass media at his disposal but he hasn't begun to think how to use it.

He hasn't even put any significant effort into fully informing the staff of the rationale behind his proposals – How on earth can he expect them to back him? They, inevitably, see them as 'his plans'. They are, to them, merely something that affects them. Nobody knows what is going on. Plans are continuously changing and every one feels insecure.

The quality of reporting influences the way people view the organisation, but Ralph hasn't learned this lesson.

Alan fails to report

Alan Sands is not VAT registered, so he does not have to send in VAT returns, but his financial backing from PYBT is conditional upon him sending in a monthly report on his performance and cash flow.

PYBT stresses the importance of careful planning and control and the report reflects this. It tells the scheme managers whether attention to this has been adequate. They are not highly complicated reports, but they do contain considerable detail. Supported young business people cannot neglect this aspect of management and get away with it.

You will note from Chapter 3 that Alan has neglected stages 1, 2 and 3 of the report-writing process to date and so his reports are so behind schedule that he is at risk of losing his financial backing.

DISCUSSION POINTS

1. Give some examples of 'data' and 'interpretation of data'.

2. What reports have you encountered or written? How would you rate them now?

3. Do you think opinions and interpretations are basically the same thing, or is there a difference?

SUMMARY

- Records deal with data, reports deal with data + interpretation.

- Reports are necessary for planning and control, for co-ordination of different departments, and for informing interested parties of performance and development.

- Reports may be simple communications of performance or explanations of discrepancies, or they may represent highly technical investigations and advice.

- Reports should contain facts and interpretations. Where relevant, they should state alternative approaches to resolving any problem, include a conclusion and give recommendations.

- The order of the reporting process is collection of data, recording of data, analysis of data and reporting.

- The format and timing of some reports are governed by law.

- Regular and accurate reporting reduces the likelihood of corruption.

- A firm's reporting influences the way people view the firm.

5
Learning to Read Accounts

WHAT THE ACCOUNTS CAN TELL YOU

Anyone considering a financial involvement in a business, whether large or small, should treat any information given about it with caution. He should ask himself, 'Who says these are the facts – the proprietor, the internal accountants or an independent accountant? How do they know? What techniques have they used to value the stock? Has a professional valuer been employed? How have they calculated depreciation on machines and vehicles? How has goodwill been valued? Is anything missing from the information (eg possible liabilities), and if so, what?'

'Creative accounting'
Creative accounting can dress up a firm's performance and net worth to make it look better than it is. Everyone puts their best features forward, so to speak, and tries to keep dirty washing hidden. Those who are to succeed in the business world must be inclined to look beyond the veneer, at what has *not* been said. What reports *don't* say, can be more important than what they do. What they do say will be what the writers want you to know, for their benefit. What they don't say will include what they do not wish you to know, for it may put you at an advantage. It's important to know what kind of things to look for.

'Profitability'
The unseasoned entrepreneur may be highly impressed and easily swayed to become involved in a firm if it reports high profit figures. But 'profitability' is more important than 'absolute profits'. It is the percentage return on capital used that you need to look at.

Which of these firms do you think manages itself better:

| Firm A | Capital used | £500,000 | Profits | £100,000 |
| Firm B | Capital used | £3,000,000 | Profits | £300,000 |

Firm B is certainly making a much bigger profit, three times that of firm A. But Firm A is earning a much better return on its capital – 20% compared with Firm B, which is only managing to earn a 10% return.

Furthermore, one year's high profits could just be a flash in the pan. Look for comparisons with previous years and also at how the profits compare with other firms in the same industry.

People find it confusing that a company's profits are not reflected in its bank balance. It could have made record profits, for example, yet its bank balance ended up in the red. To explain this, you need to see a **statement of sources and application of funds**. This shows changes in the bank balance in terms not only of profit, but of all the other inflows and outflows of funds, for example concerning stock, plant or premises, creditors and debtors.

Cash flow and solvency

A firm should have enough assets in cash, stock and debtors to be confident it can pay its bills when they become due and continue to fund its activities. It's not sufficient simply to have a pound in stock and 'bills owed in' for every pound of 'bills owed out'. The world is full of surprises. Customers often don't pay on time and sometimes people won't buy your goods however hard you try to persuade them. But creditors don't tend to accept 'surprises' as an excuse for not paying. As a general rule of thumb, current assets (stock, debtors and cash) should match current liabilities (bills to be paid within the next year) in the ratio of 2:1, but this will vary according to conditions.

Of course, in the final event, it's the flow of cash that's most important to a firm – banks and other lenders will certainly be more concerned with this than with profits. Cash to a firm is what air is to a human being; profit to a firm is what achievement is to a person. Nobody would put achievement before air.

But holding too much cash is throwing away profit opportunities, for cash in hand or on current account doesn't earn interest. So you have to balance one thing with another, keeping enough in cash or 'near cash' form (cash, stock and debtors) to be reasonably sure that they will turn into cash as cash becomes needed.

It's possible that profits for the year and the closing bank balance are both high, yet **ratio analysis** shows the firm to be insolvent. It's a 'statement of working capital flow' that you need to see to explain this. It explains changes in overall working capital in terms of profit and other inflows and outflows of funds.

Net assets

The value of net assets is an important fact to discover, but this is not as straightforward as it seems. To what degree do the book values reflect current replacement costs? If they are much lower, the funds put aside for replacement may not be enough to replace them when need be. This will be the case for two reasons:

- If the profit reflects a revaluation of stock, and the latter has been included in the profits distributed to shareholders, there may not be sufficient funds left to replace stocks.

- Fixed asset values are recorded in terms of what they were at the time of purchase, and depreciation allowances are based on those values. But it may cost far more to replace them three years later, because of inflation. Therefore the amounts allocated for replacement will be insufficient.

Financial growth between one year and another may not be what it appears to be; in inflationary times the erosion of money value can be responsible for some of the difference.

Gearing and return on capital

It's important to look at the proportion of owners' equity to permanent loan capital. This is called the **gearing** of the company. A high gearing ratio means a high proportion of permanent loan capital. This represents a high risk if the firm's profits fluctuate from year to year. If long-term backers do not receive their interest payments they may withdraw their funding and the firm could end up in the hands of the receiver. In contrast, financing by owners'/ shareholders' funds demands no scheduled repayments or interest. The gearing ratio should reflect the predictability and consistency of profits year to year. If profit tends to fluctuate greatly, the firm should not fund itself too much with permanent loan capital. If profit is consistent, then it makes sense to use other people's money.

It's also important for the investor to consider the **opportunity cost**. What rate of return could he expect by placing his money in another, perhaps safer, investment?

The **return on capital employed** (ROCE) is the important measure of profitability. The trend of ROCE is what matters, not any one year's figure. An upward trend indicates rising profitability – a downward trend means the reverse, and the reasons may be in the market. The product life-cycle may be declining as the product begins to be replaced by new innovations, or the competition may be hotting up. Alternatively a falling trend may be due to a weakening control of costs and efficiency of operation. The cause of a downward trend can be found by using secondary ratio analysis.

Checking profit margins
Gross profit

Gross profit as a percentage of sales shows the relative success of the buying function – the existence and exploitation of marketing economies of scale, like bulk buying for example, or the degree of control of the market, ie the power of the firm to manipulate prices. Consequently, it indicates the strength of competition the firm has to contend with. A high level of competition forces margins down to the minimum level. Relatively high margins indicate a low level of competition.

High margins may also suggest good cost control in manufacture, so that the cost of finished goods transferred to trading account is low in comparison to that of other firms.

They may also represent a relatively high degree of selling expertise, resulting in favourable selling prices.

Net profit

Net profit is what remains from gross (trading) profit after overhead expenses have been deducted. A relatively high net profit margin as a percentage of sales suggests a relatively good control of overhead costs (vice versa in the case of a low margin).

A firm's 'asset turnover' is the efficiency with which it uses its assets. Put more precisely it's the number of times the net assets have reproduced their own value in sales revenue each year. Again, it's the trend, rather than an absolute figure, which is important, so comparisons with previous periods are important. Comparisons with other firms producing the same goods or services are also important. A once-only figure in isolation says nothing conclusive.

If the net profit as a percentage of sales is less than you would expect, the control of each individual overhead expense has to be looked at, wages, rent and electricity, for example. Similarly, if the asset turnover ratio is low, then each individual fixed and current asset must be looked at.

Asset turnover ratios

The individual asset turnover ratios are the number of times each individual asset has, with the help of other assets, generated its own value in sales revenue. Asset turnover ratios fall into two categories – fixed asset turnover ratios and current asset turnover ratios.

To give an example of a fixed asset turnover ratio, suppose £1,000,000's worth of coaches generated £2,000,000 of revenue per year from excursions. It would amount to an asset (coaches) turnover ratio of 2. It doesn't mean that the coaches alone did it, though. They had help from other assets like the main garage premises, the repair equipment, the sales office and the money in the bank. Likewise, the coach firm's garage premises may be realistically valued at £2,000,000, so the garage asset turnover would be

$$\frac{\text{£2,000,000 garage value}}{\text{£2,000,000 revenue from excursions}} = 1$$

This means the garage would have reproduced (with the help of the other assets) its own value in revenue. You can apply the same calculations to all fixed assets.

Current asset turnover ratios
These include **stock turnover** and **debtor turnover**.

Stock turnover (often referred to as simply **stock turn**) is the number of times the firm has sold its stock and replaced it, for example in a year. Stock-holding costs money for it takes up space which could be used for other, profitable activities. The longer it remains unsold, the longer before its cash value can be used to purchase more goods for sale at a profit.

Stock turnover period is also an important consideration. This is the time taken to sell the whole of the average stock level and replace it. Stocks are, of course, replaced as they are sold, so there will never (hopefully) be a point where there is none left. However, we can still discover the length of time it takes to sell an amount equal to the average stock level.

Does the stock turnover or the stock turnover period represent efficient usage of this asset? Again, this will depend on comparisons with previous periods and with other firms in the same industry in the present period.

When a firm allows its customers a credit period, this means it funds their purchases temporarily until they pay their bills. That money used to fund their purchases could have been used to generate profit in other ways, but a firm allowing a credit period regards it as good economic sense to use it to generate sales figures. The debtor turnover ratio shows the efficiency with which the funds put to this use generate sales figures, ie the number of times they generate their own value in credit sales figures. For example, a debtor turnover of five indicates there have been £5 of credit sales for every £1 owing, on average, during the year.

The debtor turnover period (similar to the stock turnover period) shows the average time it took during the year for debtors to settle their accounts. Again, we have to judge these by reference to other years and to other firms in the industry for the same year.

Solvency

The solvency of a firm is more critical than its profitability, for providing the firm has good plans and learns by its past experience, it can buy time to put them into practice. However, regardless of how good profits are, unless sufficient assets are kept in cash or near cash so that it can pay its debts when due, a firm is likely to fall into the hands of the receiver to be wound up (or bankrupted if not a limited company).

There are two signs of the solvency of a firm:

1. **The current ratio** (sometimes referred to as the **working capital ratio**). This is the current assets divided by the current liabilities. The rule of thumb is 2:1, but lesser figures than this may be acceptable provided they are justified by careful planning and control.

2. **The acid test ratio** (sometimes referred to as the **liquidity ratio**). This is the current assets other than stock divided by the current liabilities. The rule of thumb is 1:1. Individual firms may choose to maintain a slightly different ratio based on a careful judgement of their circumstances.

Interpreting share prices

Shareholders and prospective investors will be interested in the gains to be had from investment in shares. In particular, they will focus on the earnings per share, the dividend yield and the **price earnings ratio** (often referred to as **PER**).

The **earnings per share** does not give a measure of the gain in relation to the price paid. It is the **dividend yield** which gives this.

Dividend yield   *Example*

$$\frac{\text{Dividend per share}}{\text{Market price per share}} = \text{Dividend yield} \qquad \frac{3p}{75p} = 4\%$$

Again, a trend means more than a single figure, so you need to compare it with previous years' figures. A fall may not be a significant reason to avoid, or withdraw, an investment. The fall may be due to a greater percentage of profits being retained on profit and loss account or general reserve account to finance growth. This should enhance the value of the shares and also the future earnings. A fall may, on the other hand, be due to a rise in the market price of the shares. This trend, itself, is to the advantage of shareholders.

The **price earnings ratio** gives the pay-back period for an investment at the current earnings rate. In other words it indicates how long it would take for the share to pay for itself. If the share price is 70p and the earnings per share 10p, then the PE ratio would be 7. In other words, the share would in theory pay for itself out of earnings after 7 years.

THE CHECKS YOU SHOULD MAKE

Have you noticed, when your car goes wrong, the repairman follows a precise sequence of checks to pinpoint why? Mechanics aren't the only ones who use fault-finding sequences; financial managers and accountants use them, too.

Checking the return on capital

The **return on capital employed** (ROCE) is called the primary ratio. As this suggests, it is the first check to be made. If the ratio shows the return to be lower than planned, proceed to the next stage of checks – calculating the secondary ratios. They are:

- net profit as a percentage of sales

- asset turnover.

The first of these pinpoints (or rules out) the control of the production and/or trading activities and/or overhead costs as the source of the problem. The second investigates whether all or any of the problem lies in the efficiency of asset usage.

Whichever is revealed to be the general site of the problem (and it may be both) you then proceed to the appropriate branch of the tertiary ratios. They are the last in the line of checks and will reveal the source/s of the problem. The one branch contains individual expense ratios and the other individual asset turnover ratios.

If the net profit percentage is lower than it should be then the next stage is to work out each individual expense total as a percentage of sales.

Example
Wages as a percentage of sales

$$= \frac{\text{Wages}}{\text{Sales}} \times 100$$

Heat and light as a percentage of sales

$$= \frac{\text{Heat and light}}{\text{Sales}} \times 100$$

Motor expenses as a percentage of sales

$$= \frac{\text{Motor expenses}}{\text{Sales}} \times 100$$

This will pinpoint those costs which have escaped firm control.

If the asset turnover was lower than planned, you go on to calculate the relationship between each individual asset of the firm on the one hand, and *sales*, or *cost of sales*, on the other.

Checking profitability
To check the return on investment, and the cash flow, you need only the current balance sheet. However, to make the checks really meaningful you need something to compare them with, ie figures for other firms in the same sector and/or figures for the same firm in previous years. The calculations are easy:

$$\text{ROCE} = \frac{\text{Net profit}}{(\text{Fixed assets} + \text{working capital})} \times 100$$

Apart from comparing ROCE with that of other firms, and that of the same firm in previous periods, it also has to be compared with the return you would get in a super-safe investment, eg gilts or a building society savings account. If the ROCE is consistently less than this, then there are no grounds at all for investing, for greater risks must pay greater rewards.

Secondary ratios
1. Net profit as a percentage of sales (NP %) = $\dfrac{\text{Net profit}}{\text{Sales}}$ x 100

2. Asset turnover (AT) = $\dfrac{\text{Sales (S)}}{\text{Net assets (NA)}}$

Tertiary ratios
Individual expense ratios = $\dfrac{\text{Each individual expense total}}{\text{Sales}}$ x 100

Checking asset usage/asset turnover ratios

1. Sales to land and buildings = $\dfrac{\text{Sales}}{\text{Land and buildings}}$

2. Sales to plant and machinery = $\dfrac{\text{Sales}}{\text{Plant and machinery}}$

3. Sales to vehicles = $\dfrac{\text{Sales}}{\text{Vehicles}}$

Be aware that the figures can be misleading. For example, assets might only have been in the firm a month or so. Also, the full effect on sales revenue may not be expected to show itself in the first year.

Sales to current asset ratios
1. Stock turnover = $\dfrac{\text{Cost of goods sold}}{\text{Average stock}}$

Average stock is found by the calculation:

$$\dfrac{\text{Opening stock + Closing stock}}{2}$$

From this the stock turnover period can be calculated. This is the time it has taken to turn over the whole of the average stock value. You do this by dividing the rate of stock turnover into fifty-two (weeks of the year). For example, if the rate of stock turnover was five (ie the firm had sold its entire stock value five times in the year) then the stock turnover period (time required to sell the entire stock, on average) would be

$$\frac{52}{5} = 10.4 \text{ weeks}$$

2. Debtor turnover $\qquad = \dfrac{\text{Credit sales}}{\text{Average debtors}}$

The cash sales are left out of the equation, as they have nothing to do with debtors. The debtor turnover can be converted to the debtor turnover period (the average time it takes for debtors to pay their bills) by, again, dividing it into fifty-two. For example, if the debtor turnover was ten, then the debtor turnover period would be

$$\frac{52}{10} = 5.2 \text{ weeks}$$

Checking for financial vulnerability
Tests of solvency
The **current ratio** (or **working capital ratio** as it is sometimes called) is calculated by the formula:

$$\frac{\text{Current assets}}{\text{Current liabilities}} = \text{Ratio} \qquad \overset{\textit{Example}}{\frac{£800,000}{£600,000}} = 1.33$$

The formula for calculating the **acid test ratio** (or **liquidity ratio** as it is sometimes called) is:

$$\frac{\text{Current assets} - \text{stock}}{\text{Current liabilities}} = \text{Ratio} \qquad \overset{\textit{Example}}{\frac{£800,000 - £200,000}{£600,000}} = 1.00$$

Share performance checks
1. The earnings per share is found by:

$$\frac{\text{Net profit} - \text{tax} - \text{dividend on preference shares}}{\text{Number of ordinary shares issued}}$$

2. The dividend yield is:

$$\frac{\text{Dividend per share x } 100}{\text{Market price of shares}} = \text{Ratio} \qquad \frac{10\text{p x } 100}{250\text{p}} = 4.0\%$$

Example

3. The price earnings ratio is:

$$\frac{\text{Market price of shares}}{\text{Earnings per share}} = \text{Ratio} \qquad \frac{250\text{p}}{12.5\text{p}} = 20.0$$

Example

THE NEED FOR CAREFUL INTERPRETATION

You need to take great care in interpreting company figures because they can conceal things which, if known, would significantly influence any decision to become involved. Nobody can afford to make bad business decisions. The higher the risk the higher the return you should expect. So you've got to assess very carefully how much risk there really is. Profits may be very high, but they can disappear overnight along with your investment, if the gearing level is inappropriate, the cash flow out of control, or the working capital inadequate.

They might also, to some degree, be **phantom profits**, due to things like over-valuation of stocks, a careless sales policy (resulting in many uncollectable debts) and under-assessment of the bad debts provision.

Inflation may have seriously eroded the value of the fixed assets, though they are still misleadingly shown at book value in the accounts. If the provision for depreciation is insufficient to replace them when necessary, then what now looks like profit will have to be used to fund this expense later on.

CASE STUDIES

Theresa delegates

Theresa L'Pralm does not concern herself with price levels, stock levels or credit control, at least not in a direct way. She would neither have the time, nor the space in her head to do so. She would only start worrying about such things if they got out of control and deviated from budgeted levels, causing a significant cashflow problem. Then she would ask the executives concerned to explain what had gone wrong and how they propose to put it right. 'That's their job', she says. 'And if they can't do it we must appoint someone who can.'

Ralph's cash flow crisis

Ralph Elmaster's Authority has run very short of cash, since it has overspent its budget by £2 million. If the problem cannot be rectified the Authority is at risk of disbandment by the government.

The Authority has to rationalise its asset structure, and let go of some fixed assets to improve the cash flow. It is holding too much of its capital in fixed assets. A deal which has been made for the sale of three hospitals was badly planned, from the hospital's point of view, as it allowed for staggered payments, so that it didn't ease the cash flow anywhere near as much as it ought to have done.

Ralph's Authority might also consider going into partnerships to run some of the smaller hospitals so that private enterprise could provide at least some of the working capital.

Alan sticks to his customer base

Alan Sands has had neither the wish nor the opportunity to become involved in any business other than his own since he began trading. Almost all his customers are private individuals or Local Authorities and the only involvement he has had with other firms is as a sub-contractor to them on relatively small jobs.

DISCUSSION POINTS

1. List some of the many ways in which profit figures may be distorted.

2. Approximately what would you expect the stock turnover period to be of:
   (a) a small, street-corner general store
   (b) a high street jeweller
   (c) a supermarket chain like Sainsbury's?

3. Approximately what would you expect the current ratio of each of these businesses to be?

SUMMARY

- Always look behind the veneer of business accounts.

- *Profitability* is more important than absolute profit and cash is more important than either.

- You need comparatives to make any figures meaningful.

- Business accounts which look favourable on the surface may conceal looming problems such as cash flow shortages or gearing crises.

- Inflation can significantly distort the picture.

- Profits may be phantom profits.

- The firm may be vulnerable to takeover.

- Use primary, secondary and tertiary ratios to investigate the return on capital employed.

- Use current ratio and acid test ratio to assess a firm's solvency and liquidity.

- The gearing ratio reveals how much of the firm is actually owned by owners/shareholders. It shows how vulnerable the firm will be if its predicted sales do not materialise.

6
The Need to Plan Ahead

PLANNING TO MEET DEMAND

There are financial costs to holding too many fixed assets or too much stock – it represents inefficient use of resources. Equally, there are costs in holding too little – it will mean lost orders.

Demand must be predicted for each week or month and stocks of finished goods budgeted to coincide with that. In this way the firm's stock turnover period (see page 79) is kept to a minimum.

The price factor
In a free market economy what ensures the matching of supply with demand is **price**.

A number of things influence how a firm sets its prices:

Total costs of production
Direct costs plus apportioned overheads.

Planned returns
Profit levels.

Liquidity needs
How short of actual cash it is.

Competition
Supply of close substitutes on the market. These can either be the same type of product produced by other firms or different types of product which serve a similar purpose (butter/margarine).

Type of demand
Some products become more attractive as price goes up (paintings,

prestige cars, etc), but most sell faster the lower the price. Demand for some products reacts more to a change in price than others. If matches doubled in price it's doubtful that demand for them would change much, but if cars went up by even half that percentage sales would crash.

Price elasticities for particular products are known and can be expressed in index form. An elasticity of one (known as unity in demand) means when price goes up sales go down in direct proportion. An elasticity of less than one (known an inelasticity) means sales won't go down by the same proportion as prices go up, so firms will be more inclined to raise prices here. Elasticities greater than one mean that if prices are raised sales will fall at an even greater rate, so firms will be reluctant to raise prices of these goods.

However, unless you have a monopolistic or oligopolistic control of the market (significant control of supply either on your own or together with a small number of other firms) you won't be able to exploit this knowledge to raise profit margins above a reasonable level. In competitive conditions there will always be someone ready to undercut you if there's room to do so and still make a fair margin.

Size of market share sought
The larger the market share sought the greater the incentives the firm is going to have to give to customers, but such incentives are not always low prices. Indeed, they can be a double-edged sword: once you set prices low it's difficult to put them up without losing the customers you gained. Furthermore, fixing prices low is a good way of establishing an inferior image for the product. Using things like 'two-for-one' offers, 'money-off' coupons and other special offers are better (though they, too, are just price cuts in disguise).

Understanding pricing methods
There are several methods firms use to set their prices:

'Cost + ', or 'mark-up'
Adding an acceptable net profit to the average total cost of producing each unit.

Marginal cost pricing
Adding an acceptable net profit margin to the total cost of producing additional units after all the overheads have already been absorbed in production costs to date.

Variable pricing
Charging higher prices in peak periods to encourage some of their customers to use services at off-peak periods, and so match supply more closely with demand.

Price discrimination
Setting different price levels for different customers, eg half-price for children and OAPs.

Price differentials
Setting a fixed cost to cover maintenance of hired equipment and a variable unit cost to cover usage, eg telephone service.

Price searching
Trying different prices until you find the one which will maximise profits.

Corporate pricing
When aspects other than the profitability of the particular item in question are taken into account. An example is when a firm wishes to woo customers for other profitable lines by keeping prices of frequently purchased essentials low. Some retail franchises, for example, sell things like bread below cost price simply to pull customers into the store. They know they will then spend money on more profitable lines. A similar example is cut-price air fares, offered to attract customers into profitable holiday accommodation. Some firms may seek to maintain a reputation for stable prices or value for money.

Bidding for tenders
Competing against others, largely on price, for contracts to supply goods or services to a customer. In this kind of pricing, common in building contracts and dealings with Government departments, the firm must guess what prices the other contenders have offered, as the competitive bids are not disclosed. It must balance its desire to win the order with its need to make a reasonable profit margin.

PLANNING THE FLOW OF CASH

No matter how high profits the firm is making, if it does not maintain an adequate supply of cash it will go under. This could happen, for example, if it increases its credit sales and allows a debtor turnover period of six weeks, while its creditors allow only five weeks on average, or if the firm diverts some of its cash resources towards the purchase of fixed assets.

To ensure adequate cash is available when needed a **cash budget** or **cash flow forecast** is prepared. This compares the expected inflows and outflows of cash, month by month, and shows the effect on the bank balance. If it results in a shortage the firm must make an arrangement in advance for the bank to permit an overdraft, or arrange in good time some other source of funding to make up the expected shortfall.

It's important to avoid overdrawing without permission, as banks often charge punitive interest rates and charges for unauthorised overdrafts. And why shouldn't they? It's no different really from a firm charging incredible fees for unauthorised car parking on its car parks. The bank may also refuse to honour the firm's cheques.

ENSURING FINANCIAL VIABILITY

In producing any goods or services there will be some overhead costs which can't be directly attributed to production. Cost of materials, of course, will only be incurred if production takes place, but rent, heat and light in the office premises and office staff's wages will have to be paid even if it doesn't. Up to a point, then, all the revenue received over and above the **direct costs** (materials and production labour) will go towards paying the overheads.

- Only when all the overheads have been covered can any of the income be regarded as profit.

Example
Suppose a product cost £9 to produce, in terms of materials and direct labour, and sold at £20. All the surplus £11 would be swallowed up in overheads so long as production remained below break-even point.

It's important to predict that break-even point, for if predicted demand in the market-place doesn't exceed it, it would be foolish to go ahead with the project. Moreover, to take account of uncertainty a sensible entrepreneur would want predicted demand to exceed it by a margin of safety.

Calculating the break-even point
There are two ways to calculate break-even point.

First method

$$\text{Break-even level of production} = \frac{\text{total fixed costs}}{\text{contribution to overheads}}$$

Suppose total fixed costs (overheads) were £10,000, variable costs were £9 per unit and selling price £20 a unit. The break-even level of production would then be:

$$\frac{10,000}{9} = 1,111 \text{ units}$$

Second method

The other way is to use a break-even chart, plotting fixed costs (always horizontally), total costs and revenue lines on a graph. The total costs are the fixed + variable costs, so they are drawn by plotting the variable costs per unit when starting at the fixed cost line. This way the result includes both. The break-even point is where the sales revenue and total cost lines cross, and the gap between the predicted level of sales and the break-even point is the margin of safety. It's expressed as a percentage of sales.

Calculating the margin on safety

Suppose predicted sales were 5,000 units and break-even point was 2,000. The margin of safety would be calculated as follows:

$$\frac{5,000 - 2,000}{5,000} \times 100 = 60\% \text{ margin of safety}$$

AVOIDING PREMATURE SHUT-DOWNS

If sales fall below break-even point, should we shut down? No – it's not a sufficient reason to stop production.

It's unlikely that the firm's premises could be sold in the short-term anyway, so rent, or mortgage repayments, will still have to be paid. Furthermore, low sales may just be due to bad market conditions short term, and the firm might wish to try to weather the storm until things pick up again. Continuing production will result in a loss, but it may not be as big as the loss which would be incurred if no production were done at all. After all, the rent still has to be paid, the office staff can't be laid off without notice, and the firm may want to retain all or some of them. As long as the revenue from production covers the variable costs (direct labour and materials) any surplus at all will make at least some contribution

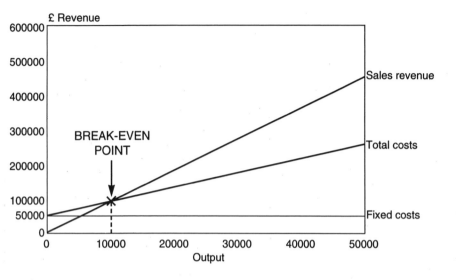

Fig. 5. Example of a break-even chart.

towards the overheads, even though it won't completely cover them. Better they're partly paid than not at all.

Since the market is governed by the forces of supply and demand, as demand decreases so will market price. Shutdown of production is not justified however until **marginal revenue** is equal to **average variable cost** ie until the price received for each new unit of production only covers the production costs and leaves nothing over to help pay the overheads if the firm intends to stay in business and keep its factories and equipment. Even if it doesn't, shutdown isn't justified before final arrangements have been made to sell the plant and equipment and lay off the staff – the firm still has to minimise the drain on its resources from rent or loan repayments, etc. If it becomes **insolvent**, however, it's legally obliged to apply for voluntary liquidation. Generally, a firm becomes insolvent when it becomes unable to pay its bills on the dates they are due to be paid.

A weakness of the break-even chart is that it doesn't take account of the 'law of diminishing marginal returns' in the production process. Up to a point the application of more units of labour and materials will increase marginal profit returns; economies of scale present themselves, such as possibilities for specialisation in manpower and bulk buying discounts in respect of materials. But

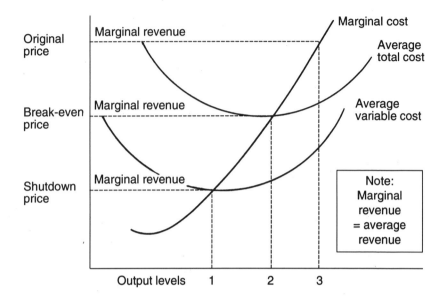

Fig. 6. Price-related break-even and shutdown points.

after a point the reverse becomes true and diseconomies begin to take place. The larger the workforce the worse the labour relations become and strikes may affect production. As the layers of supervision and management grow 'red tape' slows things down.

Secondly, as forces of supply and demand, rather than the firm, determine market price levels, falling demand will result in falling market price. This will affect marginal revenue just as units of sales will. A decision as to when to shut down production needs to take this into account too. A more accurate way to consider the shutdown point is shown in figure 6.

WHEN TO TURN BUSINESS AWAY

Absorption costing

While the best method of dealing with expected future costs is marginal costing, the best way of dealing with actual costs is **absorption costing**. This is because it's based on what has actually happened; it spreads the fixed costs (as well as the variable costs) over the whole of the actual level of production, a level which could not be foreseen with certainty. Consequently, the actual unit costs will be higher than the predicted marginal costs.

Selling below cost price
But suppose an order is offered to the firm for a number of units at a price which is below 'actual cost price', should it turn it away? If you said 'yes', then you're wrong. Don't forget that as long as it has not been sold at a loss to date then all the fixed costs have been absorbed; any price above the variable costs per unit will be all profit.

Example
Suppose the 'actual cost' of units produced by a firm is £10 per unit (made up of £4 variable cost and £6 contribution to overheads). An overseas firm, from a country to which the business does not normally export its goods, offers to buy 4,000 units at £8. Yes, it's below the £10 cost price as calculated by the historical method of absorption costing, but it would be daft to turn it away, because that cost price refers to what has already been produced. All the overheads have already been covered, so everything above the variable cost of £4 per unit is profit. You see, *absorption* costing is appropriate whenever you want to ascertain what actual costs were. *Marginal* costing is the best when you want to predict what they *will be*.

DECISIONS ABOUT ASSET PURCHASES

Asset purchases involve large investments of funds, for example to purchase:

- land and buildings
- plant and equipment
- commercial vehicles
- shareholdings in other organisations.

Asset purchases may also involve complicated choices about finance, for example the use of cash, leasing agreements or other long-term finance from banks or other institutions. Consequently, errors of judgement could have disastrous consequences. This is why these decisions are left to senior management and/or directors. Firstly, they are likely to have the best knowledge and skill to make the right decisions. Secondly, they may well be the proprietors themselves. Risk-taking is essentially their role; it's what they receive their rewards for and it's their money which is at stake.

Capital investment decisions involve a great deal of uncertainty,

much more than short-term operating decisions. The anticipated
return will be spread over a number of years and may vary over that
period. Changing political and economic conditions, including lack
of demand and inflation, will have their effect. Whatever the
uncertain return, it must be compared with the more or less certain
return which would be received in a safe investment like gilts.

There are ways that the risks can be reduced, but they can't be
removed altogether. But that's what entrepreneurship is all about;
that's what profit is for – the taking of risks. It's appropriate, then,
for such risk-taking decisions to be made by the entrepreneurs or
their most senior executives.

CASE STUDIES: FINANCIAL PLANNING

Theresa: 'Managers should manage'

Theresa L'Pralm expects her managers to control performance so
that it conforms to plans. In her view that's what they are there for.
If she had the time to do it herself why would she want to employ
them? If her managers were not capable of doing the job they are
paid for they would not have been appointed in the first place.
'You've got to delegate, and delegate all the way,' she would say.
'Then you've got to stand by your decision to appoint them and give
them their head. If they fail, the proper course is to replace them
expediently, rather than attempt to lead them by the nose. Such a
course is wasteful; it duplicates the cost of human resources, starves
the director's function of the director's time and it is disrespectful to
"wet-nurse" anyone of the calibre of a senior manager.'

Budgets out of control

Ralph Elmaster's district health authority has been rather ineffective
about controlling budgets in the past two years. Every aspect of costs
has run out of control, staff numbers have risen beyond budget, it has
been getting poor value for money from its estates department. It
would have done better to market-test the building and maintenance
services needed, as the competitive tendering process would certainly
have kept prices down. Likewise, many of the staff functions could
have been farmed out to the private sector and cost less. Where there is
no competition prices will always be high.

A simple approach for a simple business

Alan Sands prices his services at £15 per hour for labour, and trade
price plus ten per cent for materials. He carries little or no stock,

ordering as and when he needs materials and having them delivered to site if necessary.

His credit control plan at the start of his business seemed a little confused. He aimed to allow thirty days' credit on large jobs and all jobs for business customers and Local Authorities. He would insist on prompt settlement on completion for all jobs carried out for private customers. But he also planned to ask for part-payments in advance and for stage-payments throughout the course of the jobs.

The way things have actually worked out, though, is that more or less all his jobs have been for private customers and settled on completion.

Alan has few overheads, his wife dealing with his paperwork and answering the phone. He also carries a mobile phone himself. There is only his van, his equipment and his public liability insurance to cover, plus the cost of his fixed and mobile phones. He has no employees on permanent contract.

His monthly overheads he predicted like this:

	£
Insurance	150
NI	40
Loan repayments	111
Professional fees	25
Advertising	50
Vehicle tax	10
Telephone	40
Minimum level of drawings	400
Depreciation	50
	£876

Because of the nature of Alan's work it is not possible to plot variable costs linearly on a break-even chart, as you could for manufacturing. He must just ensure that monthly invoice values – less direct wages paid, materials and petrol costs – cover the monthly overheads figure he has worked out.

DISCUSSION POINTS

1. What, if any, personal experience have you had of over/understocking or of cash flow problems? What did you learn from the experience?

2. What examples can you think of, of 'variable pricing', 'price discrimination' and 'price differentials'?

3. How useful is a break-even chart?

SUMMARY

- Avoid holding too much or too little stock.

- Plan the flow of cash and prepare well in advance for shortfalls.

- Set prices carefully.

- Plot the break-even point.

- Don't be too quick to cease unprofitable production; it can make things worse.

- Use the marginal costing method to evaluate the viability of new orders.

- Capital investment decisions involve much more risk than day-to-day operational ones, and should be left to senior managers and/or proprietors.

7
Keeping Hold of the Reins

FOSTERING THE RIGHT ATTITUDES

'It's not my problem!'

It's all too easy to close your eyes to the need for financial efficiency in your firm, if you have no direct financial interest in it in the form of shares or capital. It's also commonly felt that the firm owes a secure living to its employees and, as a big enterprise, that it will be able to shoulder the responsibility. Employees are quick to jump to conclusions that they've received a raw deal when manning reductions are announced because profits are not high enough. If there are profits at all, they say, then the firm should be satisfied.

But it's not as simple as that. If profitability is less than other firms', shareholders will be dissatisfied and sell their shares. This can leave firms vulnerable to takeovers and this can soon put everyone's job at risk.

Awareness of the need for efficiency of resource usage and financial accountability has to be instilled in the whole firm, from the top down. Responsible attitudes need to be fostered at every level. Nobody *owes* anyone a living, everyone has to *earn* it.

The competitive edge

Efficiency of financial resource usage plays a crucial role in profitability. The business world is a jungle and jungle rules apply. In nature, all creatures have to compete for survival. Some increase their competitive edge by developing their efficiency of operation; others don't. Only those that do so survive, and devour those who don't. But this results in the evolution of ever more formidable players in the game, so the effort to improve efficiency and reduce waste can never let up. If you ease off, another gains the advantage. It's tough, yes, but that's life.

Firms need to make profits high enough to satisfy shareholders so that they'll keep hold of their shares, perhaps even put in more investment, and protect your livelihood a bit longer from the teeth of the predators.

Financial responsibility and willingness to stand on one's own feet and succeed or perish on one's merits has to begin at the level of individuals, for it is they who make up firms. It's tough for all the creatures of the world to survive, but in the West we've grown used to the false protection of a rather unnatural buffer from the real world – the welfare state. It was a beautiful idea, but it couldn't work for ever, because it defied the law of nature. It prevented citizens from having to go through the rough training nature puts creatures through to teach them to survive. Inevitably, citizens would prefer the protection and welfare of a safe, non-demanding state provider than the harsh conditions of the human jungle – which animal wouldn't? Though the family tabby might do a little token hunting now and again, even she will still prefer to rely on the bowl of cat food put out for her by the warm fire.

A culture of dependency

As a result, the state has nurtured an ever-growing proportion of non-survivors. This has led to a situation where those who are prepared to pit their wits, work hard and take risks are asked to support those who won't, or can't, because they have never learned how. It will reach a point where the risk-takers will say the residual rewards for risk-taking – left over after they have supported the non-risk-takers – is not commensurate with the risks, and they will no longer be prepared to take those risks to keep those who won't.

A new beginning

Now we have to undo the long process which has prevented so much of the population from developing the skills and qualities it needs to survive. In today's global markets, we have to show people the more appropriate attitudes they must develop – the willingness to take risks and responsibility for their own survival and the willingness to continuously work at improving their own competitive edge. There is no let-up, no opportunity to sit back. But why should there be? – this is the human jungle, where the unvigilant will perish. We must train ourselves to survive and succeed, especially if we are to compete with so many other nations of the world keen to seize so many of the markets, industries and services not only overseas but in our own back yard.

WHAT NEEDS TO BE CONTROLLED?

There's little point in planning, investing and organising resources in the pursuit of any goal if things are not properly controlled. Things will not automatically follow the best path to success. We can plan to the utmost degree, invest in the best resources and organise them in the best possible way, but they won't achieve the goal on their own, without fine tuning of the system from time to time. Life is much too unpredictable for that. Control is as necessary as planning. So many factors in the economy can depress sales or increase costs and we can never be sure who else is going to enter the market and depress prices as a consequence. All the following need controlling:

- cash
- credit
- costs
- stock levels

- capital gearing
- working capital
- liquidity
- share prices.

CONTROLLING THE CASH

Many people find it hard to see how a firm making high profits can be short of cash, but it can. Just as the purpose of an aeroplane is to deliver you to a destination, and an unbroken supply of aviation fuel its means of getting you there, profit is the purpose of an enterprise and an unbroken cash flow its means of achieving it. Cash flow is far more critical than profitability. An aeroplane which has lost its way, but has enough fuel to find it again, will arrive; one which is on course and ahead of time, but short of fuel will not. In the same way, a company enduring a rough ride can buy time with cash, while a firm enjoying high sales figures, but short of cash, may fail to reap the rewards. If you've got fuel (cash) you can keep the vehicle going and eventually get there; if you're short of fuel you can't.

Cash flow analysis is the technique used to discover exactly what went wrong.

Cash received
When we talk of **cash** we mean money in the bank and in the cash box (although in modern firms the latter will be just a small amount

to pay various expenses). The income which a firm receives from its trading activities can be in cash (which includes cheques) or credit, ie customers will have time to pay. They are typically given thirty days' credit, but very often take more. If a firm has a sudden profit bonanza, but all the business is on thirty day credit terms, the extra profit produces no cash at all – *at the time*.

Furthermore, suppose the firm was only able to generate that profit bonanza by selling goods cheaply, having purchased from wholesalers at reduced prices on the basis that it paid 'cash on the nail'. The firm's cash resources may well have been drained in the process. If it runs out of stock before its own customers pay their bills it will have no cash funds to replenish it.

This, of course, is an oversimplification; things are rarely this straightforward, but it does show generally how profitable firms can easily run out of cash. It's more usual that a firm's own customers are simply slower in paying their bills than the firm's suppliers allow it to be, but the effect is the same.

Running out of cash results from unsynchronised timing of costs and revenues. It can also happen if a firm uses its cash resources to pay for fixed assets, which will not generate their own value in revenue very quickly.

As a rule, fixed assets (plant, premises, equipment, vehicles, etc) should not be purchased with cash. They should be funded by loan or credit over a period equal to the assets' projected lifespan. That way at least the annual total of payments will be almost matched by what is, in effect, an income, in the form of depreciation allowance against tax. The remainder not covered in this way (ie the interest) will be offset as an overhead expense. Even here, though, there will be an imbalance between what is coming in and what is going out, for the loan or credit will probably have to be paid quarterly, or even monthly, while the effective income mentioned will only be received at the end of the year.

What a cash shortage means
The consequence of cash shortages can be:

- Unwillingness of suppliers to supply goods until the firm's accounts are settled. This prevents the firm from generating cash to 'trade its way out' of the problem. It's a vicious circle.

- Inability to pay wages.

- Inability to make repayments to financiers, eg banks.

- Use of bank overdraft will result in high interest charges.

- Expensive machinery may have to lie idle because of lack of cash for raw materials, power or fuel and production workers' wages.

- There may well be interest to pay on the loans that have financed their purchase.

- Maintenance contracts may be put at risk.

- Some depreciation cost will arise even though the machines are not being used.

- Insurance premiums will still have to be paid.

- Factory rent still has to be paid.

- Office staff's salaries still have to be paid.

The instrument for controlling the cash flow is the **cash flow forecast**, or **cash budget** as it is sometimes called. This is a table which sets out the forecasted cash requirements at particular times and matches them with the projected cash incomes, revealing any shortfalls and stating how that shortfall will be financed. A simple example is given in figure 7.

Cash flow shortages happen suddenly. By forecasting and budgeting in advance supplies of cash can be arranged in good time to make up the shortfall, by arranging bank overdrafts, factoring or new share issues, for example. In the Government's case, it borrows from the public by issuing bonds (**gilts**).

Government departments have the added problem that they may have to work within relatively fixed and apparently inadequate incomes, unlike firms whose incomes are determined by their trading activities.

First aid for cash flow problems

These are some of the remedial steps which can be taken:
- Delaying payment of bills.
- Reducing stock levels (selling off stock, purchasing less new stock).

	1	2	3	4	5	6	7	8	9	10	11	12
INCOME												
Sales	9500	10000	12000	14000	15000	15200	15500	16000	13000	14000	15000	15500
Income from other sources	200	200	200	200	200	200	200	200	200	200	200	200
(A) TOTAL INCOME	9700	10200	12200	14200	15200	15400	15700	16200	13200	14200	15200	15700
OUTGOINGS												
Purchases	3800	4000	4800	5600	6000	6080	6200	6400	5200	5600	6000	6200
Overheads	8500	7500	7500	7500	8500	7500	7500	7500	8500	7500	7500	7500
Other outgoings	0	0	0	0	0	0	0	0	0	0	0	0
(B) TOTAL OUTGOINGS	12300	11500	12300	13100	14500	13580	13700	13900	13700	13100	13500	13700
(A) – (B) NET INCOME/ OUTGOINGS	-2600	-1300	-100	1100	700	1820	2000	2300	-500	1100	1700	2000
Add opening bank balances	1500	-1100	-2400	-2500	-1400	-700	1120	3120	5420	4920	6020	7720
CLOSING BANK BALANCE	-1100	-2400	-2500	-1400	-700	1120	3120	5420	4920	6020	7720	9720

Figure 7. Example of a simple cash flow projection.

- Reducing payments to any reserve fund.
- Using factoring facilities (borrowing money on the strength of customers' accounts owed in).

When too much cash can be a bad thing

It's not only shortage of cash that can be harmful to a firm – too much cash is a drain on its productivity, because it represents the underemployment of an asset. All a firm's resources should be devoted to earning a return, and money left lying in a bank is not doing so. Furthermore, its value will be eroded by inflation. Even if interest is paid, if bank interest would satisfy the investors' demands for a return they might as well have placed the cash straight in the bank themselves.

The amount of cash maintained in a business should be enough, but not excessive.

CONTROLLING CREDIT

This is necessary for two reasons:

1. If our customers take longer to pay their bills than our suppliers allow us to pay theirs, we'll run out of cash eventually, no matter how high our paper profits are.

2. The older a debt becomes the greater the likelihood of it becoming a bad (uncollectable) debt.

One way of controlling this is by working out a regular **debtor turnover ratio** and **purchases to creditors ratio** and trying to keep the two in rough balance. This is only a partial answer, though, because if not enough control is effected on the debtor end, suppliers (creditors) will become impatient and refuse to supply goods until their bills are paid. Delay may sour the firm's relationship with them altogether, resulting in their total unwillingness to continue supplying the firm on credit. It's crucial, therefore, to keep firm control on the debtor end, to get the cash in as quickly as possible.

The debtor turnover ratio can be converted to a debtor turnover period by dividing it into 52 (to give it in weeks) or 365 (to give it in days).

Example

$$\frac{52 \text{ weeks}}{\text{Debtor turnover ratio: 8}} = \text{Debtor turnover period (6.5 weeks)}$$

$$\frac{365 \text{ days}}{\text{Debtor turnover period: 8}} = \text{Debtor turnover period} = 46 \text{ days}$$

WATCHING COSTS

Whether you're running a private firm or a government department you'll have to control costs all the time. There's no point in planning and organising your resources to produce the best return if you're not going to put the plan into action – costs won't control themselves. They can subtly rise without you realising, because few of them are as simple as they seem. Take wage costs, for example. There's not just the actual gross pay involved, there's employers' NI contributions, welfare benefits and, perhaps, the cost of providing an inflation-proof pension scheme. What if the Government suddenly increases NI contributions? What if inflation starts increasing again? It's necessary to continuously monitor costs of producing each good or service and 'tweak' them wherever necessary. This is done by **standard costing** and **variance analysis**.

Standard costs
The standard cost comprises materials, labour and a proportion of overheads. It is calculated for each unit of production, whether goods or services are being produced. Each of these component costs is worked out as follows:

Materials costs   = usage × price.
Labour costs   = hours per unit × wage rate per hour.
Overheads   = total budgeted cost for this production run
      ÷ the number of units to be produced.

Efficiency is governed by costs and output. It will increase when costs remain constant and output goes up, or when output stays the same but costs fall.

Adjusting standard cost
It's sometimes necessary to adjust standard costs, because of rising prices or errors of judgement in forecasts of the efficiency levels. Actual production costs are regularly compared with the standard costs and the variance (adverse or favourable) noted. If an adverse variance is found it has to be analysed into its constituent parts – materials, labour and overheads. Each of these, in turn, is broken down into its elements to see whether it is usage or price which has run to excess. This is called **management by exception**, because the

focus is on correcting exceptions or deviations from the planned course.

To find the value of usage variants, if any, you multiply the usage deviation by the price. To find the value of price variants you multiply the usage by the price deviation.

The problem can lie in one or more of the following:

- material usage

- material prices

- labour usage

- labour wage-rates

- number of units produced

- overhead costs.

A simple example of the variance analysis used in budgetary control is shown in figure 8.

Item	Budgeted costs £	Actual costs £	Variance £	
Materials	500,000	489,600	10,400	(F)
Labour	300,000	332,500	32,500	(A)
Overheads	60,000	61,980	1,980	(A)
Total	860,000	884,080	24,880	(A)

Fig. 8. Example of variance analysis in budgeting.

Analysed further:

Materials variance

£

Usage = Standard price x (standard quantity -
actual quantity)

= £5 x (100,000 - 102,000)   = 10,000 (A)

Price = actual quantity x (standard price -
actual price)

= 102,000 x (£5 - £4.80)   = 20,400 (F)

10,400 (F)

Labour efficiency variance
(Usage per unit)

£

Standard rate x (standard hours - actual hours)

= £5 x (60,000 - 63,000)   = 15,000 (A)

Labour price variance
Actual hours x (standard rate - actual rate)

= 65,000 x (5 - £5.269)   = 17,500 (A)

32,500 (A)

Overhead cost variance

= 1,380 (A)

Overhead volume variance

=   (Actual volume - standard volume) x $\frac{\text{standard cost}}{\text{standard volume}}$

=   (9,000 - 100,000) x $\frac{£60,000}{100,000}$

=   -1,000 x £0.60   = 600 (A)

1,980

The right attitude to budgetary control

Some people resent their performance being monitored closely in this way and see it as a conspiracy. But hopefully this chapter will show you why it is so necessary.

Successful budgetary control amounts as much to a common, fostered attitude as to a skill or technique. It means the willingness of all employees to be accountable for their performance.

Government departments will set budgets annually, known as PPBS (Planning, Programming – Budgetary Systems), in consultation with the Treasury. They will then compare their actual with budgeted performance every three or six months.

Retail firms may have major reviews of actual performance against budgeted performance every six months.

The budgetary process
The budgetary process is as follows:

1. Define the project.

2. Set realistic standards of efficiency of resource usage (materials, labour and overheads).

3. Collect data on actual performance systematically.

4. Compare budgeted with actual performance at regular intervals.

5. Take remedial action when and where necessary.

KEEPING THE RIGHT STOCK LEVELS

All the factors of production (land, labour, capital and enterprise) must earn a return. Together, they enable a firm to keep its prices to the minimum and so compete with other efficient firms. Capital tied up in stock earns nothing while it's sitting in the stock room. There are exceptions, though, such as in times of high, general inflation, or when there's a scarcity of a commodity the firm deals in (eg valuable antiques). On the other hand, the firm will lose revenue if it doesn't have stock available when customers want it and it will incur a manufacturing loss if materials are not available as and when its factory needs them. The right balance has to be struck between over- and understocking.

Other disadvantages of overstocking are as follows:

- Some stocks are perishable and overstocking will cause losses, as goods have to be thrown away.

- Some goods (especially high-tech ones) quickly become obsolete when new developments come onto the market.

- Stocks of clothes go out of fashion.

- High-tech goods tend to fall in price, so stocks would eventually be rendered unsaleable at the original prices and, in fact, may have to be sold below cost price.

In times of high inflation stock-holding can, theoretically, be advantageous, because stock values will increase. But firms often continue to sell at the listed retail prices at the time they, themselves, purchased the goods. Indeed, this policy may be required by the manufacturers. Petrol companies, however, are frequently accused of exploiting oil scarcities by setting pump prices higher, not only on the new stocks they, themselves, have had to pay more for, but also on the stocks they already had before the oil prices went up.

But we must not forget that the direct purpose of revenue from sales is to buy more stock – to keep the money circulating. You will, therefore, need more funds to do so than if prices had not gone up as a result of a scarcity.

But stock-holding is expensive. Not only is the working capital tied up in the stock, but the land and buildings required for storage also cost money in rent (or rent foregone if let to another firm). In addition, there is the heating, lighting and store-keeping labour to take into account. Furthermore, any increase in value of stock as a result of inflation will not necessarily compensate for the loss of the multiplying effect of rapid turnover and will certainly do nothing for cash flow.

Analysing stock levels

The main instrument for stock control is the **stock turnover ratio** and its derivation, the **stock turnover period**. Stock turnover is calculated by the formula:

$$\frac{\text{Cost of goods sold}}{\text{Average stock}} \quad eg \quad \frac{£480,000}{£80,000} \quad = 6.0$$

This is turned into the stock turnover period by dividing it into 52 to

find the stock turnover period in weeks, or into 365 to find it in days
eg: $\underline{52}$ = 8.67 weeks; $\underline{365}$ = 60.83 days.
  6   6

Stock turnover means the number of times during a year that the
entire average stock value has been sold and replaced. The stock
turnover period is the average time it has taken to sell and replace
the average stock.

A reasonable figure for the stock turnover period has to be
worked out based on customer or factory demand patterns, on the
one hand, and suppliers' delivery patterns on the other. Once
decided, the stock levels are planned. Of course, this measure
requires the values of 'cost of goods sold' (sales - purchases and
other selling expenses) and 'average stock':

$$\frac{opening + closing\ stock}{2}$$

It therefore requires the production of the annual, or interim,
accounts.

The stocks can then be controlled by a booking in and out system.
Periodic stock checks (half-yearly or annually, for example) can be
used to discover discrepancies and adjust the stock figures. In many
firms, such as supermarkets, a real-time computer system adjusts
stock records the moment any goods are sold, by taking electronic
data direct from the cash tills.

Stock valuation methods

The actual values of the stocks are calculated by one of three ways,
known as

- FIFO (First In First Out)

- LIFO (Last In First Out)

- Average cost method.

The most common method is FIFO, which assumes firms will
seek to sell their oldest stock first. A full treatment of these methods
is given in *How to Master Book-Keeping*, Peter Marshall (1992).

FIFO values stock at its cost price, assuming always that what
remains in stock represents the most recent purchases. The cost
prices are, therefore, those on the most recent invoices. LIFO does
the opposite. The average cost method averages out the cost of all

the stocks present every time a withdrawal is made.

WEATHERING STORMS IN ADVANCE

Businesses exist in an uncertain environment. We never know for certain what conditions will be thrust upon us tomorrow. All sorts of things can affect the environment, from competitor action on the one hand, to political or economic changes, on the other. It is wise to be prepared for rough seas in the business environment.

The trading figures of some firms are easier to predict than others. Food retailing, for example, is a safer bet than high-tech innovative product manufacturing. The lower profit margins in food retailing reflect the lesser degree of risk. If expected sales don't materialise, insufficient funds will be generated to pay interest on permanent loan capital (preference shares and debentures), if much of the firm's capital is financed in this way. Debenture holders must be paid whether the firm makes a profit or not; failure to pay could result in enforced cessation of business and subsequent liquidation.

If, on the other hand, most of the capital is from the proprietor's own funds, or made up of ordinary share capital, it's more likely to be able to keep going.

If your trading figures are highly predictable you can benefit by financing the firm with a lot of permanent loan capital (preference shares and debentures). If, on the other hand, they are highly unpredictable, it's better to finance the firm largely by the proprietor's own, or ordinary shareholders', funds. The higher the risk the greater should be the ratio of own, or shareholders', funds to permanent loan capital. The lower the risk the greater may be the ratio of permanent loan capital to owners', or shareholders', funds. This is called the **capital gearing ratio**.

KEEPING THE LIQUIDATOR AT BAY

When things get tight, when interest rates rise, for example, making overdrafts increasingly expensive, suppliers begin to enforce their credit limits more severely. Bank managers or bank policies can change overnight, with sudden demands on firms to clear their overdrafts. The firm may respond by pressing all its customers to settle their accounts, but there's no guarantee they will; some may even fold under the pressure of the new economic conditions. In the meantime your bank won't wait. If you haven't left yourself a margin for error your firm could be in trouble.

- The rule of thumb to use here is 'keep your current assets (cash, stock and debtors) equal to twice your current liabilities (creditors and bank overdraft, if any)'.

Ratios to look out for

The surplus of current assets over current liabilities is called the **working capital**. It's the fund used for buying goods and raw materials for production, and for paying overhead expenses. If working capital runs out the firm can't 'work'. The proportion of current assets to current liabilities is known as the **current ratio**; providing this is kept at an acceptable level, then if some of your customers don't pay up quickly there may be enough others who do. Similarly, if some of your stock doesn't sell quickly there may be enough other lines which do. Overall, your effort to turn your current assets into cash to pay your bills may only have worked by half, but half was enough.

If, coupled with these economic conditions, there is also a slow-down in trading figures, you will not be able to rely on selling stocks to settle the sudden demands upon your firm from creditors. For this reason it's a good rule of thumb to keep your liquid assets (cash and debtors) equal to your current liabilities in the ratio of 1:1. This is because you can't force people to buy your goods, but you can, in theory, force them to pay their debts (if they have sufficiently good credit statuses, and if they don't you shouldn't have given them credit in the first place).

Current ratio   *Example*

$$\frac{\text{Current assets}}{\text{Current liabilities}} = \text{ratio} \qquad \frac{\pounds2.4 \text{ million}}{\pounds1.2 \text{ million}} = 2$$

Acid test ratio   *Example*

$$\frac{\text{Stocks and debtors}}{\text{Current liabilities}} = \text{ratio} \qquad \frac{\pounds1.2 \text{ million}}{\pounds1.2 \text{ million}} = 1$$

If a firm becomes insolvent the managers will have to account to shareholders as to why the working capital dried up. The instrument for this is the **working capital flow analysis**. This analyses the inflow and outflow of funds and shows the difference as an increase or decrease of working capital.

KEEPING THE VULTURES AWAY

Many people wonder why business directors are so concerned about the prices of their firm's shares on the stock-market. After all, they are only second-hand shares changing hands. The firm doesn't get any of the profit when share prices rise, nor suffer any direct loss when they fall. Once the firm has issued and been paid for them they are out of their hands for the holders to do what they wish with them.

Low share prices attract asset strippers

But there's a very good reason for directors' concerns. Normally the share prices of companies closely reflect the asset values which they represent, but even on the stock-exchange, prices are determined by the forces of supply and demand. If nobody wants the shares the price drops; if everyone is rushing to buy them the price rises. If the prices drop below the underlying asset values a predatory firm can make a quick profit by buying them up, dismantling the firm and selling off its assets piecemeal. This is known as 'asset stripping'. The predator may also be getting rid of a competitor in the bargain – quite a smart move when you're even getting a profit for your efforts. That's why directors are so concerned about share prices. Takeovers can be highly detrimental to the interests of a company and its personnel; they can lead to thwarted prospects and wholesale job losses.

So how can directors keep share prices up 'buoyant'? Well, prices will fall if nobody wants them. People buy and keep shares because they out-perform others in terms of dividends and share-price increases (dividends are share-outs of profit). They are less concerned that such companies spread their risk by diversification, because they, themselves, will do that, but they do evaluate the stability of the firm and the predictability of its performance. The return they will expect will be based on that.

This explains why firms sometimes have to make the unpopular decision to reduce manning levels. Unions argue that there is no justification for sacking people if a firm is making a profit at all, but it's not just *any* level of profit that will do. If its profits are not high enough to enable it to pay dividends equal to those of other firms, shareholders will sell their shares, prices will fall and the firm will become vulnerable to takeover – then everyone could lose their jobs. Three ratios used for assessing share performance are given on page 80–81.

CASE STUDIES: KEEPING HOLD OF THE REINS

Using ratios to examine a possible takeover

Theresa L'Pralm's colleague has drawn her attention to an investment opportunity of purchasing the controlling interest in a bus company. The company has been enjoying high profits for the past two years, but has run into a cash crisis. The proposal has been tabled for the next board meeting.

Theresa looked first to see if the cash crisis could easily be resolved. The acid-test ratio revealed its creditors exceeded its cash and debtors in the ratio of 1.5 to 1. The problem seemed to have arisen because one of its main customers went into liquidation owing it a considerable amount of money. The debt had had to be written off so there was no way of recovering any of it to speak of.

However, the bus company's net assets were still worth significantly more than the asking price for the shares which represented them. On further investigation, though, it was found that 15 of the 20 buses in the firm's fleet were nearing the limits of their projected lifespan and were in the accounts at cost. Prices had risen considerably since they had been purchased. It would require a large investment for their replacement and finance would be hard to obtain for the firm in the circumstances, especially as, coupled with the cash flow problems, the company had a highly geared capital structure. Consequently, Theresa decided she would not support any resolution to make an offer.

A major management challenge at the health authority

Ralph Elmaster has lost control of the District Health Authority in every way. His staff are not with him, the finance is out of control, and the buildings are falling to pieces.

Times have become much tougher of late for health authorities. Efficiency has to be improved to maintain even the level of health care there is at the present.

It is unlikely that staff will ever be completely happy about any changes which affect their pay, conditions of work, or the security of their jobs, but enough consensus to make things work may be achieved if they fully understand the need for such changes, to save 'their' Authority. You have to make it 'their plan' too, and that is what Ralph has failed to do. Instead of staff seeing the Authority's plan as primarily a threat to their jobs they need to understand that it is lack of efficiency that has posed the threat. A good indicator of a health service's efficiency is its waiting lists and Ralph's Authority has one of the longest there is. It is spending far more than the budgeted costs for the planned level of services and still not delivering them. You don't need to be a financial genius to see something is wrong.

The penalties of failing to plan

Alan Sands prepared a detailed business plan before commencing his business – he had to, it was a condition of his PYBT support. He strayed from the plan early on, though. The plan seemed no more than a paper exercise to obtain the funding.

The capital funding arranged was late coming, so a lot of early revenue was lost. In his own words, not being used to handling money, Alan used much more of his sales income as personal drawings than he had planned. He also purchased a mobile phone and used it unsparingly, so that actual telephone costs well exceeded those budgeted for. His efforts to go and look for work were not producing the results he planned for. Rather than rethink and amend his strategy he began to give way to despair. Only now is it fully dawning on him that things will not control themselves – you have to *make* them work to a viable plan.

DISCUSSION POINTS

1. Give some examples of what can go wrong with well thought-out financial plans.

2. Have you, or anyone you know, ever had business cash flow problems? If so, how did they arise, and what eventually happened?

3. Do your colleagues generally understand the real meaning of profits?

SUMMARY

- Things won't control themselves.

- All plans need fine-tuning from time to time, because not everything can be allowed for.

- Cash is more critical than profit and has to be carefully controlled. The cash levels should not be more or less than is necessary.

- Cash flow problems arise from unsynchronised costs and revenues.

- Shortages of cash result in high interest rates, as overdrafts have to be used and, at worst, may result in the firm being unable to continue producing or trading. The effect will be made worse by the fact that overhead costs will continue to run despite no revenue coming in.

- Plan for expected cash shortages well in advance.

- Do not pay for fixed assets with cash or other kinds of working capital. Use longer-term funding instead.

- Make sure colleagues understand the real reason high profits are so important.

- Be prepared to give unyielding attention to improving efficiency and foster this attitude among colleagues.

- Instil the personal accountability ethic into all colleagues.

'Plan for expected cash shortages well in advance.'

8
Investing in the Future

MAINTAINING PRODUCTIVE CAPACITY

It's quite reasonable to argue that if people aren't buying, the goods shouldn't be produced. But what if the lack of demand is only temporary?

- During a slump, productive capacity lying idle will deteriorate. It may not be worth repairing by the time demand picks up again. Specialised machines take a long time to make and to fit. A laid-off labour force will have to be replaced with other workers, and they can't be recruited and trained overnight.

- A more insurmountable problem may be the decline of the firm's product image and market share. Much of a product's value today is in the form of intangible, associative values – emotional experiences, or perceived identity. (Think of branded products such as Coca Cola, or pop music CDs.) It takes time to build up a valuable image in the minds of the public and if that image remains out of people's consciousness for too long it will be forgotten. Moreover, the firm's old customers will begin to satisfy their needs with another, close substitute, product. The firm will have lost its market share.

Market penetration (breaking into market shares of other firms) is a difficult and costly process. It means developing a unique product image from scratch. This will involve a lot of advertising and that means a great deal of money.

Handling an investment dilemma like this is a matter of personal judgement. There are grave risks whatever you do. But the problem must be faced squarely, and decisions made on firm economic criteria, rather than taking the easy way out and avoiding the issue until it's too late.

PLOUGHING BACK PROFITS

A firm's productive capacity can also be diminished if too much of the profit is taken out and not enough ploughed back to replenish assets and finance growth. On the other hand, if too much of the profit is ploughed back shareholders will become dissatisfied because they're not getting as big a dividend for their money as they would if they held shares in some other company instead.

Directors have to walk this tightrope, for if they overdo the reinvestment the company can lose in two ways at once:

1. The shareholders may become dissatisfied with their dividends. They may sell their shares, share prices will fall and the company could quickly become vulnerable to takeover and perhaps asset stripping.

2. If the reduced dividends have been caused by reinvestment of profit to enhance the firm's assets then a predatory firm would be even better rewarded for its takeover – because of the increased assets the shares would represent.

The fact that a firm has reinvested profits to sharpen its competitive edge may to some degree assuage the dissatisfaction of shareholders, who might then hope for higher dividends in the future. Many shareholders seek a quick return, though, and are not prepared to wait for long-term rewards. The longer into the future that returns are delayed the more uncertain those rewards become anyway.

Two methods of ploughing back profits
There are two ways in which some of the profits are held back to finance growth:

1. They are simply retained as a **profit and loss account balance brought forward.**

2. Transferred to **general reserve account.**

A nation's need for productive capacity
Maintaining the capacity to produce is important at a national level, too. Importing more than it's exporting will lead a country into a 'balance of payments' problem. The Government has to balance what it's importing with what it's exporting.

If the country's industrial structure is to remain adequate, and indeed grow so that its industries can compete with foreign firms and so protect British jobs, its infrastructure of highways has to be maintained and improved. But how far will the increasingly overburdened taxpayers be prepared to stand the cost, at least directly, through taxes? There will, at least, be pressure to increase efficiency of resource usage in order to keep the tax burden to the minimum.

Subsidies
Should a country subsidise key industries in times of world recession to prevent the run-down of their factories? If they fall into decay foreign firms will snatch their market shares once things pick up and then we've got another balance of payments problem.

But who's going to pay for such subsidies? They won't grow out of thin air; they have to come from taxpayers, or from borrowing on taxpayer's behalf. In times of recession people's enthusiasm and confidence to invest are low and are dampened further by overtaxing earnings and company profits. For firms it also means giving assistance with one hand and taking it back with the other, not to mention making it harder for some firms (the unsubsidised) and easier for others (the subsidised). As for the alternative, government borrowing tends to run at a high level in times of recession anyway, and governments are more concerned to keep it down than let it increase.

INCREASING OUR COMPETITIVE EDGE

In addition to competing in the home market, businesses also have to compete against foreign firms. In the Third World companies have low labour costs and can often compete strongly. Some industrialised countries have highly automated industries – the Japanese, for example.

It's not simply a greedy plot to cheat the workers out of a fair day's pay for a fair day's work, or of their jobs by substituting them with machines. If foreign firms haven't paid their production workers at such levels, however low they may be, or if they've used more automation, then however much they regret it, firms here will have to cut their pay levels and substitute machines for labour too. It's the only way they can compete on price.

Workers whose jobs are at risk because of aggressive global competition are not going to stop buying cheaper foreign goods themselves. They're not going to dip their hands deeper into their pockets and buy the British goods, more expensive because they carry greater labour costs. We can't really complain, then, when the failure of British goods to sell leads to job losses and wage cuts. We can't have it both ways. Indeed, if firms didn't take measures to sharpen their competitive edge it wouldn't just be some, it would be all their workers that would end up 'on the dole'.

The firm's competitive edge has to be continually sharpened at another face too – its dividends. Trade unions may say there's no justification for firms to lay people off if they're making profits at all. But 'any old' profits won't do. Profits have to be comparable with others in similar industries; otherwise the shareholders will sell their shares and buy those of another firm instead. Share prices will fall and this could lead to a takeover, with all the risks to jobs that entails.

A continued effort is needed by both firms and individuals to improve their competitive edge all round, making themselves stronger and fitter to survive. The other players in the game will be doing so and they won't be making any allowances for weakness – it's not that kind of game.

FORESEEING THE NEEDS OF THE FUTURE

Governments have to look into the future to assess what will be required so that they can plan and prepare in advance. This means identifying trends. For example, there are increasingly more live births and infertility is almost a thing of the past. More and more children are surviving their infancy, and more and more people are living longer.

Social changes
The poverty of unemployment leads to an increasing crime rate and this is exacerbated by the increasing population of elderly people, who are highly vulnerable to petty crime. Increasing demands on the police force, the courts and the penal reform institutions are a fact of life.

Energy needs
With the growing switch to automated production, necessitated by aggressive competition from foreign companies, more and more electrical and fossil fuel energy will be required. In addition, the overworked soil on our farms needs ever more treatments with nitrogenous fertilisers to rejuvenate it; the production of these is itself an immensely energy consuming process.

On the other side of the scales our coalfields are fast running out of economically exploitable coal and we are having to rely more and more on natural gas and nuclear power. Nuclear power is essential to keep electricity cheap enough for the production process, for it's relatively cheap to produce. However, atomic energy plants are vastly expensive to build. Planning and preparation has to be done years in advance and plant construction takes many years.

It's not only governments which must look into the future to assess what needs there will be. Firms, too, must gaze into the crystal ball. The image of the future becomes ever more obscure as the rate of change speeds up, but since tooling-up (building factory premises and installing machines) takes time firms must maintain a piercing vigilance on the future if they are not going to miss the boat when wants and needs change.

SEEING THE HIDDEN COSTS

But it isn't only the future needs and ways of satisfying them that governments must try to foresee. For every benefit there's always a cost (or costs) and the one must be weighed against the other.

The fumes from the old coal-fired power stations played havoc with people's chests. Nuclear power promises to solve our energy problems cheaply without this, but it carries it own kind of health hazards. Some authorities have associated it with increased incidence of leukaemia. Then there's the long-term problem of storing hazardous waste.

Enhanced road networks will make travel easier and will help firms cut their costs and be more competitive. But there will be more noise and pollution which will cause increased physical and stress-related disease, not to mention environmental damage.

The range of costs for each benefit is infinite. We'll probably go on discovering new hazards associated with each and every product as long as we continue using them, and perhaps beyond. As they become known their effects can be estimated in terms of hard cash.

Building a nuclear power station, or a new flyover system, will damage the health of local people to some degree and that means extra health care costs. Similarly, privatisation of a Local Authority provision, such as a local bus service, may give better value for money to users and taxpayers, but it's likely to result in reduced staffing. The effect must be converted into hard cash in terms of unemployment benefit, and probable social costs in terms of crime and illness. The increased drain on law enforcement and health care funds must also be taken into account.

Cost/benefit analysis

The technique used for weighing benefits against costs is called **cost/benefit analysis**. Put simply, it involves comparing all the direct financial costs plus all the hidden 'social' costs expressed in financial terms, on the one hand, with all the direct financial and hidden 'social' benefits on the other.

But the technique is not without its problems. It's often difficult to identify those who will pay (or suffer) the costs and those who will gain the benefits of any project. Also, the actual values of costs and benefits are difficult to assess, especially as they only become clear over time – who knows what a pound will really be worth in ten years? For this reason a **discounted cash flow** technique is used in conjunction with cost benefit analysis.

DECIDING WHICH ASSETS TO INVEST IN

The key facts to consider in any investment decision are the risk and the return. If new products are involved – beware, only around eighty per cent of such investments succeed.

Understanding the 'opportunity cost'

As for the returns, don't go for a 'profitable' investment until you've considered the opportunity cost, in other words, what you'd get if you invested your funds in a very safe investment like 'gilts' or a building society account instead.

- Deduct the opportunity cost from the expected rate of return. The difference is a reason for deciding, or deciding not, to invest elsewhere, but not before making a few other checks.

Example: investing £100,000 for one year

Expected return on investment, say:	£30,000 (30%)
Opportunity cost (building society interest @ 6%)	£6,000
Net real return on investment	£24,000 (24%)

So, after taking into account the opportunity cost, the net return on the proposed investment is 24%, not 30%. (But this may still be a good deal.)

Another way to take opportunity cost into account is to apply a **discount factor** – equal to a typical safe-investment compound interest rate – to the future returns, in order to find their 'net present value'. The net present value means what sum loaned out, or invested safely, today would give you that value at that time in the future. That's the return you're actually getting for the real business risk you are taking. There are discount tables available to provide the figures to use.

Using the pay-back method

Investment considerations often begin with a crude comparison of how long projects will take to pay for themselves. The further into the future we are looking, the more uncertain things become. The pay-back method shows the degree of uncertainty involved, by indicating how far into the future we have to wait to get back all the money invested. This method is particularly important when the firm's solvency margin is slim. The trouble is it doesn't take account of what returns there will be after projects have paid for themselves. There are better methods to help us make the best choices.

Using the average rate of return method

This works out the rate of return on the average capital employed over the lifespan of the asset. The average capital employed is calculated by:

Formula

$$\frac{\text{Initial asset value} + \text{residual asset value at the end of lifespan}}{2}$$

Example

$$\frac{£100,000 + £20,000}{2} = £60,000$$

Some firms simply use the initial capital expenditure in the calculation, rather than taking account of depreciation. The average return is worked out by adding the forecasted profits over the asset's lifespan and dividing by the number of years involved. It is then expressed as a percentage of average capital employed.

The trouble with this is that it doesn't take account of the timing of returns. For example, an investment of £5,000 expected to produce profits of £1,000 each year for five years would give the same *average* rate of return as one which produced only £500 a year for the first four years but £3,000 in the fifth. Clearly, however, the first of these is worth much more, because the earliest returns will already be earning interest in a bank or other investment. It's obviously more valuable to have your large amounts earning interest for long periods, and your small amounts earning interest for short periods, than the other way round.

Using the internal rate of return (IRR)

The technique that overcomes this weakness is the calculation of the 'internal rate of return'. This is the most commonly used of investment appraisal techniques. It converts the expected returns to compound interest rate equivalents. **Compound interest** means interest on capital and interest on the interest, too. The formula for calculating it is:

$$a = p (1 + r)^t$$

where a is the accumulated value, p the initial sum invested, r the rate of interest and t the number of years the investment is to run. When you work out the internal rate of return you are, in effect, applying the formula in reverse.

To begin with you list the expected annual returns and then, by trial and error, you find a discount rate in the tables which, when applied to each of the annual returns, will, in total, bring you back to your initial investment.

Suppose a project required an investment of £10,000 and was expected to produce cash inflows over five years of £1,500, £3,000, £3,500, £4,500 and £5,000, making a total of £17,500 over its lifespan. First we have to find the approximate internal rate of return it will provide. We can do this by deducting the initial investment from the total cash inflow, dividing the difference by the number of years and then expressing the answer as a percentage of half the initial outlay.

Example 1

Year	Cash inflow
1	£1,500
2	£3,000
3	£3,500
4	£4,500
5	£5,000
Total cash inflows	£17,500
Less initial investment	£10,000
Return on investment	£7,500 ÷ 5 (number of years) = £1,500

£1,500 expressed as a percentage   =   £1,500
of half the initial investment   ---------   × 100 = 30%
                                        £10,000 ÷ 2

We can use this as a starting point to try other rates in the table that will bring us even closer.

Example 2

Year	Return £		Discount rate 30%		Discounted return £
1	1,500	x	0.769	=	1,153.5
2	3,000	x	0.592	=	1,776
3	3,500	x	0.455	=	1,592.5
4	4,500	x	0.350	=	1,575
5	5,000	x	0.269	=	1,345
					7,442

Example 3
Too little, so let's try eighteen per cent.

Year	Return £		Discount rate 18%		Discounted return £
1	1,500	x	0.847	=	1,270
2	3,000	x	0.718	=	2,154
3	3,500	x	0.609	=	2,131
4	4,500	x	0.518	=	2,331
5	5,000	x	0.437	=	2,185
					10,072

This brings us as near as we need to be to the exact initial investment figure (only 0.1% out). It tells us that the internal rate of return (IRR) from the project will be eighteen per cent.

FINANCING THE REPLACEMENT OF ASSETS

It's easy to think that when you've purchased and paid for an asset the expenditure problem is out of way. Unfortunately, this is not the case. From the moment the asset goes into service, whether it be a machine, a motor car or anything else, it starts to wear out. To make things worse, in the climate of increasing technological change, it also begins to go rapidly out of date. If a firm doesn't update its equipment before competitors do, those competitors will gain the competitive edge by producing goods more cheaply or better.

Provision for funding a replacement has to be made from the word go. This is done by charging the annual erosion of value (depreciation) against the profit and loss account: regardless of how much profit the firm makes this erosion of value is a loss to be set against it. It's not right that the firm should be taxed on all the original profit, for taxation is only due on profits *after all costs*. Therefore the accumulation of these charges for erosion of value (together with any residual or scrap value obtained when the asset is finally sold) should in effect claw back all the money originally spent on the machine. The organisation can, therefore, use it to buy a replacement.

It may, or may not, have to pay more for any updated version, depending on price trends. A replacement computer, for example, may well cost less than the original model.

ALLOWING FOR THE EROSION OF MONEY VALUES

A project may sound very simple. If a building project is going to cost £100,000 to build, but will produce total net profits over the ensuing five years of £200,000, on the face of it, it doesn't seem a bad idea. But a fifth of that profit (£40,000) won't be coming in until year five. And how do you know what £40,000 is really going to be worth by then? Inflation erodes the value of money and we can never accurately predict the rates of inflation that will affect the economy.

Allowing for the opportunity cost
Added to this is the opportunity cost – the interest we will have forsaken by not getting that £40,000 until year five. If we had

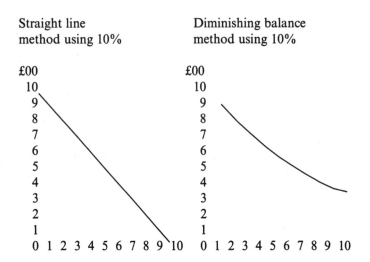

Fig. 9. Two common methods of accounting for depreciation of fixed assets. The figure of 10% is used in both cases to illustrate the comparison (it is not necessarily the most common percentage to be used).

received it at the beginning of year one, when the initial investment was made, we could, perhaps, have achieved eight per cent or so per year on it in a very safe investment. Compounded, this would amount to £18,773 or almost forty-seven per cent by the end of year five.

Allowing for future inflation

The previous kind of erosion can be worked out quite well by 'discounted cash flow' techniques (see p122), but the inflationary effect is a different kettle of fish. We can only base our estimates on how well we believe the government of the day is in controlling it.

Inflation causes other problems for firms too:

● Cash becomes a drain on profits because it loses its value.

● Stock values may rise as a direct result of inflation and this will appear to swell profits. But if the company distributes part of these swollen profits to shareholders it won't have the funds to replace the stocks when they are used up. On the other hand, shareholders may be dissatisfied with what seems a low share-out of profits.

- Fixed asset values on the balance sheet become under-stated in inflationary times and the depreciation allowed against tax become inadequate to replace them when necessary.

- Being in debt has advantages in inflationary times. The rate of interest is often less than the rate of inflation and the gain aspect doesn't show up in the balance sheet, because the assets purchased remain at cost price. But this makes it difficult to assess the growth of a firm or compare its performance between one period and another. The Accounting Standards Committee has published a number of guidelines called **Statements of Standard Accountancy Practice** (SSAPs) to try to deal with the problems of inflation.

HOW TO FINANCE NEW INVESTMENT

In the private sector the larger the firm the more sources of finance are available to it. Public companies can fund their expansion by selling new shares and issuing debentures (loans), but partnerships and sole proprietors have to rely mainly on personal funds, bank loans and credit.

The basic sources of finance
The sources of finance are either internal, or external to the firm.

Internal sources of finance
- owners' or shareholders' funds

- reinvested profit

- depreciation

- sale of existing assets.

External sources of finance
- bank loans

- leasing

- hire purchase

- credit

- debentures

- mortgages

- Investors In Industry III (source of finance available to small firms)

- BOS (income support scheme for new entrepreneurs)

- Prince's Youth Business Trust (grants to young, new entrepreneurs).

Checking the capital gearing

The gearing of a firm means the proportion of owners' or shareholders' equity to long term loan capital (eg debentures and preference shares). The gearing ratio is used by lenders and shareholders to measure the vulnerability of a firm. It has for long been held as the rule of thumb in the UK that debt (long term fixed interest loans) should not exceed fifty per cent of the total of a firm's capital (gearing ratio of 1:1), but attitudes to this are being relaxed because of low costs of borrowing. Nevertheless, gearing should still reflect the predicted ability to pay the interest on loan capital. So while, if trading figures are highly predictable, loan capital may be allowed to exceed the fifty per cent mark (high gearing); if they are highly unpredictable it should be a lower percentage (low gearing).

Furthermore, the equity proportion (owners' or shareholders' funds) should at least equal the fixed assets and some of the working capital. Financing the fixed assets with loan capital means the firm won't be able to use those assets as security to raise further funds.

Interest cover

Also the proportion of loan capital should not be so great that the firm is unlikely to earn enough to cover the interest charges five or six times over each year out of its profits. For example:

Profits before interest and taxation	£60,000
Interest charges	£15,000

(interest cover 6 times)

Advantages of high gearing
- Debt costs the company less than equity. Shareholders will expect a greater return through dividends than lenders through interest, as they're taking a bigger risk. After all, they will not receive any return at all if profits are not high enough.

- Profits will be shared among fewer shareholders, so each will receive more.

Disadvantages of high gearing
Lenders are relatively unwilling to lend to highly geared companies.

- Highly geared companies are vulnerable, as they may not be able to pay the interest on loans on time.

- The behaviour of highly geared firms will be influenced by the need for quick turnover and this may not be in their long-term interests.

Two useful ratios used for measuring proportion of shareholders' or owners' equity are:

$$\frac{\text{Equity}}{\text{Fixed assets}} \quad \text{and} \quad \frac{\text{Equity}}{\text{Total net assets}}$$

The latter will reveal the level of gearing.

Subject to the firm's existing gearing, the funding for individual investments should be repayable as far as possible over the entire, estimated lifespan of the assets involved. This way all the repayments can be funded by tax relief on profits in the form of depreciation costs; the interest will be reclaimed from tax as an overhead expense.

When all these factors have been taken into account it's likely to be the relative cost of each alternative source of finance which will be the deciding factor.

How government finances its investments

Governments rely mainly on taxation, in one form or another, and borrowing, to finance their investments. Sources of funding for investment by government, local authorities and public corporations are:

Direct taxation

- Income tax

- Corporation tax

- Capital gains tax

- Capital transfer tax

- Petroleum revenue from North Sea oil.

Indirect taxation

- VAT

- Customs and Excise duties.

Direct and indirect taxes place the burden of public financing on different sectors of the community. Direct taxes tax incomes at source, so everybody pays (subject to some allowances). Indirect taxes tax funds only when spent, and place the burden on the poorer sectors of the community most, as they have to spend all their money, while those more wealthy do not.

Other sources of revenue for governments are council taxes, rates, vehicle licence duty, national insurance contributions and shares of the profits of nationalised industries.

Borrowing to invest

The other main source of public expenditure financing is borrowing. This it does by issuing **loan stocks** – certificates (IOUs) for money borrowed, on which interest is payable over the period of the loan. These stocks or bonds can then be bought and sold on the stock market. As the bonds change hands each new owner is entitled to the interest payments attaching to them; the resale prices rise and fall according to what other more or less profitable alternative investments are available at the time.

Direct and indirect taxation

The demands on the taxpayer are becoming ever greater. The income tax rate is lower than it has been for decades, but remember that's not the only tax we pay. VAT is *higher* than it has been for decades, and there are many other kinds of taxes, too (eg national insurance, council tax, road tax, and many more). Because of the increasing burdens on the taxpayer's purse new ways of financing public works and services are having to be found. Privatisation of roads is already under way, as is privatisation of hospitals, schools and prisons. This shifts the burden from those who are forced to pay to those who pay by choice, ie those who choose to finance the goods and services on the basis of a reward for their risk. Advantages of this are:

- That it's preferable to previous methods where taxpayers had to both finance the project whether they liked it or not, and also accept the risks of the use of their money being a failure.

- Entrepreneurs are more practised and skilful in risk-taking. In their hands, there is less chance of projects doomed to failure ever getting off the ground.

- When the losses or rewards for risk fall upon private pockets, efficiency of operation is greater than if it falls on the public purse (which affects nobody directly).

CASE STUDIES: INVESTING IN THE FUTURE

Theresa's board assesses the options

Some of Theresa L'Pralm's fellow directors believe that tourism in Northern Italy will become a growth area in the next few years. The board has been considering three alternative investment projects, among them a hotel in that area. The investment required was £6 million and it would generate an estimated £7.5 million profit over 5 years. The other two projects were a coach firm in England and a leisure park in Aberdeen, each of which required an investment of £4 million. The coach firm would generate an estimated £3.6 million over 5 years and the Scottish leisure park an estimated £4 million.

Theresa pointed out that the political and economic situation in Italy is relatively unpredictable; fluctuating exchange rates add to the uncertainty. But her colleague pointed out that uncertainty is related to 'payback period'. The Italian hotel would pay for itself in 4 years whereas the coach firm and the leisure park would both take at least 5.

Another colleague, who favoured the coach firm, pointed out that the 'payback period' was only a rough guide for choosing between investments. The hotel offered the lowest 'average rate of return' of the three projects, the coach firm the highest.

The financial director then pointed out that the beauty of the leisure park was that it offered the highest profits in the earliest years. Aberdeen was one of the very few places in Europe not feeling the pinch of recession, because of its buoyant oil industry. Workers were affluent there. Coupled with this the area would be hosting two big international events over the next two years which would bring a huge amount of tourist trade. Other firms would jump on the bandwagon, but it would take them a couple of years to become established and by then 'the party would be over'. The peak trade would have gone and competition would be fierce for what was left. The equipment would cost more and more to maintain as it got older, but in the early years returns should be very high. The internal rate of return is by far the most meaningful measure of investment appraisal, he reminded them, and the leisure park exceeded both the other two alternatives in this respect: 26% as opposed to less than 24% on either of the alternatives.

The board voted in favour of the Scottish leisure park project.

Ralph weighs up the costs and benefits of health care

Ralph Elmaster is aware that health care needs are going to grow as the population lives longer, surviving more and more illnesses and infirmities. He is also aware that health care increasingly involves high tech, high cost equipment. GPs now control their own budgets and send their patients where they get the best value for money. At the same time the authority's funds are more impoverished than ever before, due to the massive overspend in recent years. To top it all, many of the hospital buildings are falling into decay, because of lack of proper maintenance.

Ralph's solution is to concentrate future funding on just the three largest hospitals in the county, sited in the three largest towns and cities. He plans to close down the other 14 and sell the buildings to the private sector. The revenue from the sales will, he believes, pay for the expensive equipment required and for major extensions to those three hospitals in terms of bed space.

There will be hidden costs in this plan, though. There will be the transportation of patients from all over the county; and what about the long-stay, elderly and mentally ill patients who presently occupy the smaller hospitals? These can, he argues, be accommodated by the private sector which, he hopes, will buy up the hospital buildings. This doesn't solve the problem at national level, but it helps reduce the burden on his authority's funds, as the DSS will pick up the bill for these patients.

Alan relies on gut feeling

Alan Sands made some bad investment decisions early on in respect of equipment he bought. He did not calculate the returns his assets (power saw, cement mixer, etc) would bring him. He decided to buy them simply because common sense told him they would save him labour costs.

His van often let him down with engine failure and lost him no end of time. If he had appraised more carefully the return he would get on the investments in equipment he'd have postponed such purchases until his firm had grown somewhat, and spent the money on a more reliable van instead.

So far he has not ploughed any profits back to finance expansion, even though he planned to do so. Nor has he made any provision for replacement of assets; he has relied instead on the residual value, when he finally sells them, being enough for a deposit in an HP agreement.

Alan is due to have a meeting with his PYBT adviser shortly who will be pointing these things out.

DISCUSSION POINTS

1. How well do you think the country has maintained its capacity to produce throughout the recent recession?

2. What do you think some of the nation's future needs will be?

3. What new ways can you think of to fund services now provided by the state?

SUMMARY

- Production decisions are more complicated than simply producing if demand is there.

- Decide carefully how much profit to plough back.

- Keep improving the competitive edge.

- Assess carefully the needs of the future.

- Government departments have to take into account social (hidden) costs and benefits as well as the directly financial ones.

- Investment appraisal techniques pay-back method, average rate of return, internal rate of return and cost/benefit analysis can improve decision-making.

- Make adequate provision for replacement of assets, from the word go.

- Remember that cash in the future will probably not be worth what it is today.

- Get the gearing right between shareholders' funds and any borrowings.

- New ways of funding welfare provisions are having to be found.

Checklist of Skills for Financial Management

Skill	Experience gained
1. Book-keeping	
2. Break-even analysis	
3. Controlling a budget	
4. Calculating asset value depreciation	
5. Controlling cash	
6. Cost/benefit analysis	
7. Controlling costs	
8. Costing (absorption)	
9. Costing (marginal)	

Skill	Experience gained
10. Credit control	
11. Financial planning	
12. Interpreting accounts	
13. Interpreting share prices	
14. Investment appraisal	
15. Pricing	
16. Report-writing	
17. Stock control	
18. Stock valuation	

Glossary

Speaking the language of finance

Accounting ratios. Statistical measures taken from the accounts of a business to aid financial assessment and control.

Accruals. Expenses incurred, but not yet billed to the firm.

Add-back. Adjustments made in the taxation computations adding non-allowable expenditure included in the accounts on to the profit for the year so that it suffers tax.

Advance Corporation Tax (ACT). A liability to tax due following the payment of a dividend by a limited company.

Amalgamation. Joining two firms into one.

Assets. All items of property and equipment owned by the business, plus money owed to the business by customers etc; money with bankers and cash held by the business (contrast **liabilities**). The term comes from the word 'assez', meaning 'enough'. It is used because the property of a proprietor is judged in terms of whether it is enough to pay off his liabilities, ie to settle his debts. Assets are classified into **fixed assets** and **current assets.** The former are those which will be retained in the business, eg machines, motor vehicles, etc. The latter are those intended to be consumed in the business within the fiscal year and includes stock, debtors, cash in hand and cash at bank. Something can be seen as an asset because it will save a future expense (eg: an insurance pre-payment) or because it will generate future revenue (eg stock).

Auditor. An external auditor is an independent consultant whose role it is to check that the final accounts give a fair and defensible view of the affairs of the company, that the legal requirements have been met and to try to ensure that conventional accountancy practices are used. Limited companies must appoint an external auditor by law. An internal auditor performs a similar role, but in practice has a little less independence. An internal auditor also recommends improvements in accounting systems and carries out spot checks on stocks.

Average cost method. A method of stock valuation in which remaining stock values are averaged out every time a withdrawal is made.

Bad debts. Debts which a firm regards as uncollectable.

Balance. This term is used in 3 different ways in double entry bookkeeping.

1. For the debit and credit column totals.
2. For the balancing item required to equalise the two column totals. (balance c/d).
3. For that balancing item transferred as the opening figure for the subsequent accounting period (balance b/d).

Balance sheet. A summary of all the assets and liabilities of an organisation at a particular time. (It is not, as some think, called a balance sheet merely because it balances.)

Bank reconciliation. A standardised format statement explaining a discrepancy between the bank statement balance and the cash book balance.

Bankruptcy. The stage when an individual's liabilities exceed his assets and his creditors are unwilling to wait for payment.

Bill of exchange. A payment document, taking the form of a post-dated cheque, which is widely used in commerce.

Bought ledger. That division of the ledger which contains personal (named) accounts of suppliers. It is also sometimes referred to as the purchase ledger or creditors account.

Break even. The stage reached when the income from a project covers the expenditure on it.

Capital. The excess of assets over liabilities which belongs to the owners of a business. It should not be confused with **working capital**, which has a different meaning.

Capital gains tax. Tax due on the profit from the sale of a capital asset.

Capital introduced. Money or other assets introduced into a business by the proprietor.

Cash. Money in the bank or in the tin/safe.

Cash book. A book used to record either bank or cash transactions. Normally the left page (debit) is used to record receipts whilst the right page (credit) is used to record payments.

Cash flow. Simply the 'flow of cash' in and out of a business. A **cash flow statement** is a schedule showing the budgeted receipts and payments for the forthcoming year. Often there is provision to include the actual amounts received and paid alongside the budgeted figures so managers can monitor the results.

Company. A business concern with a legal identity of its own and which limits the liability on its shareholders, for its debts. A company may be private (Ltd), with two or more shareholders, or public (Plc), with seven or more shareholders. Its affairs are regulated by the various Companies Acts.

Contract hire. A form of leasing.

Corporation Tax. A tax on a company's profits – effectively the corporate equivalent of income tax.

Creditors. People or companies to which you owe money.

Debenture. A legal charge over a company's assets.

Debtors. People or companies who owe you money.

Depreciation. An accounting adjustment to the assets in the books of account, made to reflect their reducing value over time.

Dividends. Shares of profit paid to shareholders.

Drawings. The retrieval of capital by a proprietor or partners for private use.

Early settlement discount. A discount offered to customers as an enticement to pay their bills on time.

Equity. The element of assets 'owned' by shareholders calculated by deducting the liabilities from the assets. The same as **shareholders funds**.

Expenses. The cost of goods or services to be consumed by the business within the financial year. They do not enhance the value of any fixed assets though they may include repairs to them. Examples are: wages, repairs, heat and lighting costs, petrol and professional fees. Sometimes called **overheads**.

Factoring. A means of raising money now against invoices due for payment over the coming months.

FIFO. First In First Out.

Final accounts. The revenue accounts and balance sheet of a firm at a particular moment in time and covering a particular financial period, eg a financial year.

Fixed assets. Property and equipment owned by the business which will have a long lasting benefit to the business, eg land, buildings, plant, vehicles and equipment.

Floating charge. The same as a mortgage debenture – a charge which 'hovers' over the assets of a company. The value rises and falls as assets move in and out, until the charge is called up at which stage it crystallises.

Freeports. Ports where goods may be off-loaded and re-shipped without customs duties and documentation restrictions.

Gearing. The ratio between the amount of assets a company has, and the amount of its borrowing limits.

Going concern/gone concern – the two bases of valuing a company. A 'going concern' basis values assets on a full market valuation, whilst a 'gone concern' basis only uses values likely to be achieved in a liquidation auction, usually minimal.

Goodwill. The intangible fixed asset of a business's reputation.

Gross profit. Sales revenue minus cost of sales. The profit earned by a business from manufacture and trading, prior to the deduction of overhead expenses. That is to say sales less direct cost of sales equals **gross profit**. (See also **net profit**.)

Gross profit margin. Gross profit as a percentage of sales.

Guarantee. A legal agreement whereby an individual agrees to settle someone's or some company's liabilities if called upon to do so.

Historical cost. The original cost, particularly applicable to fixed assets, without any adjustment for inflation which will have changed the purchasing power of money.

Imprest system. A system of managing petty cash in which a fund is regularly replenished to a set amount by the cashier.

Income and expenditure account. A non profit-making club's equivalent of a business's profit and loss account.

Indemnity. Essentially the same as a guarantee for lending purposes.

Input tax. VAT paid to a supplier on goods or services it has supplied and which the business will later recover from HM Customs and Excise.

Insolvent. The situation when a company's liabilities exceed its assets – ie if it sold everything it would still owe money.

Intangible asset. An asset, such as film rights, or goodwill, which has a worth to the business on a going concern, but which is unlikely to carry a value in the event of a liquidation.

Interest. The cost of borrowing money.

Interim accounts. Revenue accounts and balance sheet drawn up at intervals more frequent than each financial year and used for management purposes.

Invoice. A document listing goods or services supplied and showing the date, the price, any VAT, and the total amount due.

Invoice discounting. The same sort of arrangement as factoring, but usually bigger figures are involved with fewer debts.

Journal. A book of prime entry used to record adjustments and other non-recurring accounting entries. However, some people refer to the day books as journals too, eg sales journal, purchase journal, etc. and the journal as defined above is then referred to as the 'journal proper'.

Lease. An arrangement whereby an asset is rented for a specific period.

Ledger. The heart of a double entry accounting system. It consists of a number of divisions, eg the general ledger, personal ledger, cash book and petty cash book. Since each of these divisions is often kept in a separate bound book it is not surprising that people tend to think of them as separate ledgers, but this is not truly the case, they are all divisions of the one ledger system.

Liabilities. Financial obligations to others — debts owed out (contrast **assets**). Capital too is listed under liabilities in the balance sheet since it is owed to the proprietor by the business.

LIFO. Last In First Out. A method of stock valuation based on the assumption that the earliest cost prices prevail.

Limited company. A business entity which has its own rights and obligations under the law. Its capital is divided into shares and the liability of the shareholders in the event of a liquidation is limited to the value of shares held.

Liquidation. The winding up of a company – all the assets are liquidated and creditors paid (as far as possible).

Liquidator. The person nominated to deal with a liquidation.

Liquidity. The ability of a firm to pay its debts.

Merchant bank. A bank which concentrates upon large specialist lendings, share dealings and Stock Exchange flotations. Also called an investment bank.

Mortgage. A legal charge or property as security for a loan.

National insurance. A system of insurance run by the government into which workers and employers make regular payments and which provides money for people who are unemployed, old or ill.

Net profit. Gross profit minus overhead expenses. It is the bottom line figure – what is left after all deductions – and is quoted as either pre-tax, or post tax. (See also **gross profit**.)

Off balance sheet funding. A way of obtaining assets for business use, when neither the funding nor the asset feature in the balance sheet – for instance equipment leasing.

Ordinary shares. Shares in a company. In the event of a liquidation ordinary shareholders are the last in line when the proceeds of the asset sales are being distributed. See also **preference shares**.

Output tax. VAT charged to customers by a business and which it will have to subsequently remit to HM Customs and Excise.

Overdraft. A lending facility intended for day to day trading needs, to be used when needed on a fluctuating basis.

Overheads. Money spent regularly to keep the business running. Overheads include such charges as rent, heat and light, bank interest on overdrafts and other **expenses** which are not directly related to the purchase or manufacture of the goods or services being sold by the business.

Partnership. A business owned and run by two or more individuals with a view of profit. Unlike a limited company the business is not a separate legal entity from those that own it; the individual partners are jointly and severally responsible for the debts of the business. (Contrast **limited company** and **sole trader**).

Petty cash book. The book of prime entry in which records of small cash transactions are kept.

Post. To make entries in a ledger to complete the double entry recording of a business transaction.

Postage book. A book in which records of stamps purchased and used are made.

Preference shares. The same as ordinary shares except that in the event of liquidation preference shareholders are paid out before ordinary shareholders.

Private limited company. A limited liability company whose share dealings are restricted and cannot be quoted on the stock exchange. It only has to have two shareholders, one secretary, and one director to comply with company law, though that director could not also act as company secretary.

Profit. The reward to the proprietor, partners or shareholders for the business risk they have taken.

Profit and loss account. An account summarising the income and expenditure of a business for a given period and showing the surplus income (profit) or deficit (loss).

Profit and loss appropriation account. That part of the revenue accounts of a partnership or limited company which explains how the net profit is to be appropriated.

Promissory note. A commercial IOU.

Provision for bad debts. A suitable provision (allowance) set against the value of debtors to allow for some which will become uncollectable.

Provision for depreciation. An allowance set against an asset for wear and tear.

Public company. A limited liability company (Plc) which can sell its shares freely and have them quoted on a stock exchange. It must have a minimum of 7 shareholders and 2 directors.

Purchase day book. A book of prime entry in which the initial record of purchases is made before posting to the ledger.

Purchase returns day book. A book of prime entry in which the intial record of goods returned to suppliers is made before posting to the ledger.

Receipts and payments book. The main accounting book used by many club stewards in non-profit making clubs.

Receivership. The personal form of a liquidation – affecting individuals and non-incorporated bodies. The receiver handles the administrative work of the receivership.

Revenue accounts. The set of accounts which shows the net profit earned by a business, how it is calculated and how it is to be distributed. Typically they include the trading account and the profit and loss account. For a partnership or limited company they will also include an appropriation account, for a manufacturer they will include a 'manufacturing account' and for a club an income and expenditure acccount.

Revenues. Inflows of money or money's worth to the firm, eg sales figures, rents, discounts received etc. They must be distinguished from proceeds of sale of fixed assets, which is capital income rather than revenue income and is ultimately shown in the balance sheet rather than the trading, profit and loss account.

Risk capital. Money injected into a business as a long term investment in a speculative venture.

Sales day book. The book of prime entry in which the initial record of all sales is made before posting to the ledger.

Sales ledger. That division of the ledger which contains personal accounts of customers. Sometimes referred to as the debtors ledger.

Sales return day book. The book of prime entry in which the initial record of goods returned by customers is made before posting to the ledger.

Security. The provision to a lender of a legal charge over some form of asset (eg buildings, stock, debtors) enabling him to sell the asset to repay the borrowing if all else fails.

Share. A stake in the capital of a company entitling the holder to a proportion of the profits.

Shareholders funds. The value of a company's assets after deducting all outstanding liabilities.

Sole proprietorship. An unlimited firm owned solely by one person.

Sole trader. A person running a business on his own; that is without any business partner. He is personally responsible for the debts of the business.

Statement of affairs. A description and valuation of the assets and liabilities of a business and the way the net assets are represented by capital at a particular moment in time. In effect, it is the same as a balance sheet.

Stock. Goods for resale or for use in a manufacturing process for the production of goods for resale.

Stock exchange. A market which trades in the purchase and sale of public company shares.

Suspense account. An account into which a value equal to an error can be posted temporarily in order to make the books balance while the source of the error is being sought.

Taxation computation. A schedule showing the adjustments to the accounts profit in order to arrive at the taxable profit of the business.

Trading account. That section of the revenue accounts which explains the calculation of gross profit.

Trial balance. A listing and summing of all the ledger balances at a particular moment in time to confirm that the total debits equal the total credits and so provide some measure of confidence in the book-keeping.

Turnover. The amount of business done in a particular period. It is generally expressed as a measure of sales: for example £10,000 per year would mean that the total sales in one year amounted to £10,000.

Uncleared effects. A cheque will take usually three days after paying it in to be sure that it has been paid and will not be 'bounced'. During this period the amount of the funds relating to the cheque are referred to as 'uncleared effects', and usually will not be available for drawing against.

Unlisted Securities Market. The baby brother of the London Stock Exchange – a market for the sale and purchase of smaller company shares.

Value Added Tax. A tax (currently at $17\frac{1}{2}\%$) levied on the sales/supplies made by a registered trader. Because of the set-off of tax charged to the trader on his purchases the result is to collect from him tax on the value added by him.

Venture capital. Similar to **risk capital** – long term financial help to support a new (usually) unproven venture, sometimes involving equity options.

Working capital. The difference between current assets and current liabilities.

Further Reading

BOOKS

Anderson, Peter (1991), *Bank Lending: A Practical Introduction*, Northcote House.

Blake, J. (1991), *Accounting Standards*, Pitman.

Davies, B. & Ellison, L. (1989), *Local Management of Schools*, Northcote House.

Davies B. & Ellison L. (1990), *Managing the Primary School Budget*, Northcote House.

Drury, C. (1988), *Management and Cost Accounting*, Chapman & Hall.

Harlow, Gwen (1992), *How to Master GCSE Accounts*, How to Books.

Harper, W. M. (1989), *Management Accounting*, Pitman.

Hill, D. A. and Rockley, L. E. (1990), *The Secrets of Successful Financial Management*, Heinemann.

Howard, L.R. (1988), *Auditing*, Pitman.

Marshall, P. (1992), *How to Master Book-Keeping*, How To Books.

Taylor, Peter (1994), *How to Keep Business Accounts*, 3rd ed., How To Books.

Taylor, Peter (1994), *How to Manage Budgets & Cash Flows*, How To Books.

White, Dr J. (1994), *How to Invest in Stocks & Shares*, 2nd ed., How To Books.

PERIODICALS

The Financial Times, 1 Southwark Bridge, London SE1. Tel: (071) 873 3000. *The Financial Times* newspaper and magazine group also publish the following magazines: *Investors Chronicle, Money*

Management, and *The Banker*.

Business International Money Report (weekly), Economist Intelligence Unit, 40 Duke Street, London W1A 1DW.

Cash Management News Chief Financial Officer (monthly), Eurostudy Publishing Co. Ltd, 9-13 St Andrews Street, London EC4A 3EA.

Corporate Money (fortnightly), Centaur Communications, St Giles House, 50 Poland Street, London W1.

Credit Control (monthly), MCB University Press, 62 Toller Lane, Bradford, W. Yorks.

European Finance Director (quarterly), Harrington Kilbride Plc, The Publishing House, Highbury Station Road, Islington, London N1 1SE.

Finance Journal (quarterly), MacMillan Magazines, 4 Little Essex Street, London WC2R 3LF.

Financial Adviser (weekly), Financial Times Magazines, Greystoke Place, Fetter Lane, London EC4A 1ND.

Financial Director (monthly), VNU Business Publications, 32-34 Broadwick Street, London W1A 2HG.

International Finance (quarterly), Howson Leach Publishing Ltd, Upper Street, London N1 0YN.

International Finance Review (weekly), IFR Publishing Ltd, 11 Fetter Lane, London EC4A 1JN.

International Trade Finance (fortnightly), Financial Times Business Information, 126 Jermyn Street, London SW1Y 4UJ.

Key Business Ratios (annually), Dun and Bradstreet Ltd, Holmers Farm Way, High Wycombe, Bucks.

Money Management (monthly), Financial Times Magazines, Greystoke Place, Fetter Lane, London EC4A 1ND.

Money Matters (annually), The Publishing Team Ltd, 1 Hatton Street, London NW8 8PL.

Money Week (weekly), EMAP Media, 33-39 Bowling Green Lane, London EC1R 0DA.

Moneyfacts (monthly), Moneyfacts Publications, Walshams House, Stalham, Norwich NR12 9AH.

Moneywise (monthly), Berkeley Magazines Ltd, Berkeley Sq, London W1X 6AB.

Public Enterprise (quarterly), LGC Communications, 122 Minories, London EC3N 1NT.

Small Company Investor (monthly), Start Enterprises Plc, 4 Wallace Road, London N1 2PG.

Trade Finance and Banker (monthly), Euromoney Publications Plc,

Nestor House, Playhouse Yard, London EC4V 5EX.

The Venture Capital Report Guide to Venture Capital in the UK and Europe (biennially), Venture Capital Report Ltd, Boston Road, Henley-on-Thames, Oxon RG9 1DY.

Useful Addresses

Chartered Association of Certified Accountants, 29 Lincolns Inn Fields, London WC2A 3EE. Tel: (071) 242 6855.

Chartered Institute of Bankers, 10 Lombard Street, London EC3V 9AA. Tel: (071) 623 3531.

Chartered Institute of Management Accountants, 63 Portland Place, London W1N 4AB. Tel: (071) 637 2311.

Chartered Institute of Public Finance & Accountancy (CIPFA), 3 Robert Street, London WC2N 6BH. Tel: (071) 895 8823.

Finance & Leasing Association, 18 Upper Grosvenor Street, London W1X 9FD. Tel: (071) 491 2783.

Institute of Chartered Accountants in England & Wales (ICAEW), Chartered Accountants Hall, Moorgate, London EC2P 2BJ. Tel. (071) 628 7060.

Institute of Chartered Accountants in Ireland, 87-89 Pembroke Road, Ballsbridge, Dublin 4. Tel: Dublin 680400. Also: 11 Donegall Square South, Belfast BT1 5JE. Tel: Belfast 321600.

Institute of Chartered Accountants of Scotland, 27 Queen Street, Edinburgh EH2 1LA. Tel: (031) 225 5673.

Institute of Taxation, 12 Upper Belgrave Street, London SW1X 8BA. Tel: (071) 235 9381.

Index

How to Keep Business Accounts
Peter Taylor (3rd edition)

The third fully revised edition of this easy-to-understand handbook for all business owners and managers. 'Will help you sort out the best way to carry out double entry book-keeping, as well as providing a clear step-by-step guide to accounting procedures.' *Mind Your Own Business.* 'Progresses through the steps to be taken to maintain an effective double entry book-keeping system with the minimum of bother.' *The Accounting Technician.* 'Compulsory reading.' *Manager, National Westminster Bank (Midlands).* Peter Taylor is a Fellow of the Institute of Chartered Accountants, and of the Chartered Association of Certified Accountants. He has many years' practical experience of advising small businesses.

176pp illus. 1 85703 111 8.

How to Master Book-Keeping
Peter Marshall

Book-keeping can seem a confusing subject for people coming to it for the first time. This very clear book will be welcomed by everyone wanting a really user-friendly guide to recording business transactions step-by-step. Illustrated at every stage with specimen entries, the book will also be an ideal companion for students taking LCCI, RSA, BTEC, accountancy technician and similar courses at schools, colleges or training centres. Typical business transactions are used to illustrate all the essential theory, practice and skills required to be effective in a real business setting. Peter Marshall BSc(Econ) BA(Hons) FRSA FSBT MBIM has been Tutor in Education at the University of Lancaster and Director of Studies at the Careers College, Cardiff. He has contributed regularly to *FOCUS on Business Education.*

176pp illus. 1 85703 022 2.

How to Manage Computers at Work
Graham Jones

Most books on computers are highly technical, and often tied in to one particular application or product. This book really is different. Assuming no prior knowledge, it is a practical step-by-step guide which puts the business needs of the users first. It discusses why a computer may be needed, how to choose the right one and instal it properly; how to process letters and documents, manage accounts, and handle customer and other records and mailing lists. It also explains how to use computers for business presentations, and desktop publishing. If you feel you should be using a computer at work, but are not sure how to start, then this is definitely the book for you . . . and you won't need an electronics degree to start! 'Bags of information in a lingo we can all understand. I strongly recommend the book.' *Progress/NEBS Management Association.* Graham Jones has long experience of handling personal computers for small busines management and is Managing Director of a desktop publishing company.

160pp illus. 1 85703 078 8.

How to Master Business English
Michael Bennie

Are you communicating effectively? Do your business documents achieve the results you want? Or are they too often ignored or misunderstood? Good communication is the key to success in any business. Whether you are trying to sell a product, answer a query or complaint, or persuade colleagues, the way you express yourself is often as important as what you say. With lots of examples, checklists and questionnaires to help you, this book will speed you on your way, whether as manager, executive, or business student. Michael Bennie is an English graduate with many years' practical experience of business communication both in government and industry. He is Director of Studies of the Department of Business Writing of Writers College, and author of *How to Do Your Own Advertising* in this series.

208pp illus. 0 7463 0582 6.

How to Master Public Speaking
Anne Nicholls (2nd edition)

Speaking well in public is one of the most useful skills any of us can acquire. People who can often become leaders in their business, profession or community, and the envy of their friends and colleagues. Whether you are a nervous novice or a practised pro, this step-by-step handbook tells you everything you need to master this highly prized communication skill. Contents: Preface, being a skilled communicator, preparation, researching your audience, preparing a speech, finding a voice, body language and non-verbal communication, dealing with nerves, audiovisual aids, the physical environment, putting it all together on the day, audience feedback, dealing with the media, glossary, further reading, useful contacts, index. Anne Hulbert Nicholls BA(Hons) PGCE was a Lecturer in Communications and Journalism in a College of Education for 14 years and now runs seminars and conferences for a publishing company. She has also worked in Public Relations and for BBC Radio.

160pp illus. 1 85703 097 4.

How to Pass That Interview
Judith Johnstone (2nd edition)

Everyone knows how to shine at interview — or do they? When every candidate becomes the perfect clone of the one before, you have to have that extra 'something' to raise your chances above the rest. Using a systematic and practical approach, this How To book takes you step-by-step through the essential pre-interview groundwork, the interview encounter itself, and what you can learn from the experience afterwards. The book contains sample pre- and post-interview correspondence, and is complete with a guide to further reading, glossary of terms, and index. A Graduate of the Institute of Personnel Management, Judith Johnstone has been an instructor in Business Studies and adult literacy tutor, and has long experience of helping people at work.

128pp illus. 1 85703 118 0.

How to Do Your Own Advertising
Michael Bennie

This book is for anyone who needs — or wants — to advertise effectively, but does not want to pay agency rates. Michael Bennie is Director of Studies at the Copywriting School. 'An absolute must for everyone running their own small businesss . . . Essential reading . . . Here at last is a practical accessible handbook which will make sure your product or service gets the publicity it deserves.' *Great Ideas Newsletter (Business Innovations Research).* 'Explains how to put together a simple yet successful advertisement or brochure with the minimum of outside help . . . amply filled with examples and case studies.' *First Voice (National Federation of Self Employed and Small Businesses).*

176pp illus. 0 7463 0579 6.

How to Write a Press Release
Peter Bartram

Every day, newspapers and magazines are deluged with thousands of press releases. Which stories make an editor sit up and take notice? Why do some press releases never get used? The author knows from more than 20 years' first-hand experience in journalism what turns a release from scrap paper into hot news. This book takes you through every stage of the process from conceiving the story idea, researching the information and writing the release, to distributing it by the most effective means. If you have ever had a press release rejected – or want to win 'free' column inches for your organisation – *How to Write a Press Release* is the handbook for you. Peter Bartram BSc(Econ) is one of Britain's most published business writers and journalists, with more than 2,500 feature articles and seven books to his credit. He edits the magazine *Executive Strategy.*

160pp illus. 1 85703 069 9.

How to Write a Report
John Bowden (2nd edition)

Communicating effectively on paper is an essential skill for today's business or professional person for example in managing an organisation, staffing, sales and marketing, production, computer operations, financial planning and reporting, feasibility studies and business innovation. Written by an experienced manager and staff trainer, this well-presented handbook provides a very clear step-by-step framework for every individual, whether dealing with professional colleagues, customers, clients, suppliers or junior or senior staff. Contents: Preparation and planning. Collecting and handling information. Writing the report: principles and techniques. Improving your thinking. Improving presentation. Achieving a good writing style. Making effective use of English. How to choose and use illustrations. Choosing paper, covers and binding. Appendices (examples, techniques, checklists), glossary, index. John Bowden BSc(Econ) MSc has long experience both as a professional manager in industry, and as a Senior Lecturer running courses in accountancy, auditing, and effective communication.

160pp illus. 1 85703 124 5.

How to Manage People at Work
John Humphries

'These days, if a textbook on people management is to succeed, it must be highly informative, reliable, comprehensive – and eminently user-friendly. Without doubt, *How to Manage People at Work* is one such book. Written in an attractive style that should appeal to any first-line manager who has neither the time nor the energy to cope with heavy reading, John Humphries has tackled his extremely wide subject ably and well. Rightly or wrongly, it has always been my experience that one has only to read the first couple of pages of any textbook on people management to discover whether or not the author enjoys an empathy with the people at the sharp end – and here is one author who, for my money, has passed the test with flying colours.'
Progress/NEBS Management Association.

160pp illus. 1 85703 040 0.

How to Conduct Staff Appraisals
Nigel Hunt (2nd edition)

Managers and organisations neglect staff appraisal at their peril today. But what exactly is staff appraisal? Is it something to be welcomed or feared? Why is it now so vital, and what are the benefits? Should senior as well as junior staff undergo appraisal, and how could this be done? Which managers should do the appraisals, and how should they start? This book, now in a new edition, sets out a basic framework which every manager can use or adapt, whether in business and industry, transport, education, health and public serices. Nigel Hunt is a consultant in occupational testing, selection, appraisal, vocational assessment, and management development. He is a Graduate Member of the British Psychological Society, and Associate Member of the Institute of Personnel Management. 'Informative . . . Points for discussion and case studies are prominent throughout . . . the case studies are highly relevant and good'. *Progress/NEBS Management Association.*

154pp illus. 1 85703 117 2.

How to Manage a Sales Team
John Humphries

The quality of a sales team can be crucial to the success or otherwise of an organisation, especially in the fiercely competitive marketplace of the 1990s. Written by a highy experienced training professional, this book meets the need for a practical handbook for every manager responsible for building or leading a sales team. With its useful checklists and case studies, it covers the whole subject from initial planning to recruitment, sales training, motivation and supervision, controlling budgets and forecasts, running sales meetings, and managing the sales function successfully within the organisation as a whole. John Humphries BSc has 19 years' professional experience as a management trainer.

160pp illus. 1 85703 079 6.

How to Employ & Manage Staff
Wendy Wyatt

This easy to use handbook will help all managers and supervisors whose work involves them in recruiting and managing staff. Ideal for quick reference, it provides a ready-made framework of modern employment practice from recruitment onwards. It shows how to apply the health & safety at work regulations, how to handle record-keeping, staff development, grievance and disciplinary procedures, maternity and sick leave and similar matters for the benefit of the organisation and its employees. The book includes a useful summary of employment legislation plus a range of model forms, letters, notices and similar documents. Wendy Wyatt GradIPM is a Personnel Manager and Employment Consultant.

128pp illus. 0 7463 0554 0.

How to Know Your Rights at Work
Robert Spicer MA

Written in clear English, this easy-to-follow handbook sets out everyone's rights at work whether in an office, shop, factory or other setting. It outlines the legal framework, the general duties of employers and employees, the legal scope of 'employment', the contract of employment, pay and deductions, hours of work, absences from work, disciplinary and grievance procedures. Other chapters explain the law of redundancy, union involvement, what happens on the transfer of a business, guarantee payments, redundancy pay, sex and racial discrimination, the rights of expectant mothers, disabled people and past offenders. Health and safety at work is also summarised, and the book is complete with a section on going to an industrial tribunal. Robert Spicer MA(Cantab) is a practising barrister, legal editor and author who specialises in employment law.

141pp illus. 1 85703 009 5.

How to Counsel People at Work
John Humphries

The value of counselling has become much better recognised in recent times, as a tool for addressing a whole variety of human situations. This new book has been specially written for everyone wanting to know how to make use of counselling techniques. It discusses what is counselling, the role of the counsellor, communication skills, body language/verbal behaviour, styles of counselling, managing counselling interviews, and the uses of counselling. The book is complete with helpful checklists, case studies, self-assessment material and points for discussion, key addresses, glossary and index.

128pp illus. 1 85703 093 1.

How to Start a Business from Home
Graham Jones (3rd edition)

Most people have dreamed of starting their own business from home at some time or other; but how do you begin? The third edition of this popular book contains a wealth of ideas, projects, tips, facts, checklists and quick-reference information for everyone — whether in between jobs, taking early retirement, or students and others with time to invest. Packed with information on everything from choosing a good business idea and starting up to advertising, book-keeping and dealing with professionals, this book is essential reading for every budding entrepreneur. 'Full of ideas and advice.' *The Daily Mirror.* 'This book is essential – full of practical advice'. *Home Run.*

176pp illus. 1 85703 126 1.

How to Buy & Run a Shop
Iain Maitland (2nd edition)

The retail sector is notorious for the number of small shops which fail in their first few years. This step-by-step guide offers hard-hitting advice on running a retail shop, how and where to trade, records and accounts, employment and consumer law, tricks of the trade, and is complete with case studies and references. 'Before going any further, consider his advice.' *Daily Express: Business Plus.* 'Meets a real need for a practical guide for anyone thinking of buying or running a shop. With its clear step-by-step approach it sets out all your need to know to get started.' *Independent Retailer Magazine.*

156pp illus. 1 85703 056 7.

How to Buy & Run a Small Hotel
Ken Parker

'How I wish we'd had proper advice before we took the plunge!' is a frequent cry amongst those providing serviced accommodation. This informative guide meets that demand, and provides a firm base of knowledge on which to enter this competitive business. How to prepare yourself, how to decide what to look for, how to raise finance, where to get professional advice, how to select the right equipment and staff and how to run a hotel at a profit are just some of the key topics comprehensively and expertly covered. 'Also of value to those already involved.' *Business Executive Magazine/ABE.* Ken Parker is an experienced hotelier, freelance journalist and writer, and has extensive experience of managing staff, administration and lecturing.

206pp illus. 1 85703 050 8.

How to Sell Your Business
Robert Ziman

Are you thinking of selling your business? Perhaps you feel it is time for a change, or retirement beckons, or your personal circumstances have changed. Whatever the reasons, you will certainly want to get the best deal. But how do you market a business? What about the timing, method and costs? What about confidentiality, and negotiating with prospective buyers? Written by a business transfer agent with a lifetime's experience, ths book shows you step-by-step how to manage the whole process from the beginning, through setbacks, and towards a satisfactory outcome. It is complete with many examples, checklists, sample documents and other essential information to set you on your way.

160pp illus. 1 85703 119 9.

How to Invest in Stocks and Shares
Dr John White (2nd edition)

This book has been specially updated to help and guide those with a lump sum or surplus income to invest and who are considering investing all or part of this in quoted securities. Dr John White, an Oxford graduate, is himself an experienced investor and adviser to an investment company. He has a professional background in computers and has produced a range of software for chart analysis. 'User friendly . . . Contains many practical examples and illustrations of typical share-dealing documents. There are also case studies which give you a feel for your own inclinations about risk versus profit . . . Demystifies the world of stocks and shares.' *OwnBase.* 'Will be a help to private investors. . . Gives an easy to understand guide to the way the stockmarket works, and how the investor should go about setting up a suitable investment strategy.' *What Investment.*

208pp illus. 1 85703 112 1.

How to Retire Abroad
Roger Jones

Increasing numbers of people are looking for opportunities to base their retirement overseas — away from many of the hassles of life in the UK. This book meets the need for a really comprehensive and practical guide to retiring abroad — from the initial planning stages, to choosing the right location and property, and adapting to a completely new environment. Such a big change in lifestyle can involve many pitfalls. Written by a specialist in expatriate matters, this handbook will guide you successfully step-by-step through the whole process of finding a new home, coping with key matters such as tax, foreign investment, property, health care, and even working overseas. The book is complete with a country-by-country guide. Roger Jones is a freelance author specialising in expatriate information. His other books include *How to Get a Job Abroad, How to Teach Abroad* and *How to Get a Job in America.*

176pp illus. 1 85703 051 6.